Activating the
NINE GIFTS
of the SPIRIT

REVEALING THE POWER & PRESENCE OF GOD

NORVEL HAYES

Activating the Gifts of the Spirit
ISBN: 978-1-6675-0919-8
Ebook ISBN: 978-1-6803-1245-4
Copyright © 2025 by Norvel Hayes

Published by Harrison House Publishers
www.harrisonhouse.com

(Formerly *Power for Living* ISBN 978-0-89274-707-2, *Holy Spirit Gifts Series* ISBN 978-0-89274-337-9, and *The Winds of God Bring Revival* ISBN 978-0-89274-375-9)

1 2 3 4 5 6 7 / 31 30 29 28 27 26 25

Contents

Foreword

In these last days, God is flinging open the doors of His divine armory, unleashing weapons forged in the fires of heaven—weapons with the power to shatter strongholds and rescue a broken, desperate generation. The gifts of the Holy Spirit are divine weapons, and it's time for the Church to rediscover them. They are heaven's answer to the battles we face, empowering us to carry out His mission with authority and impact.

Christianity was born in the blazing fires of the Spirit, ignited in the upper room when cloven tongues of fire descended, inaugurating a movement that turned the world upside down. Today, that same fire is being rekindled. The message of the enduement of the Spirit that launched Jesus' ministry (Luke 4:18) was the same message that birthed the Church: The Kingdom of God had come with power from on high (Acts 1:8). But somewhere along the way, we lost our axe head and with it our effectiveness. Today's over-organized, streamlined version of Christianity seems to have lost that original fire and luster.

Tragically, the giants of faith have become relics of the past, and with their passing, much of their fearless teachings and transformative anointings have been buried in the sands of time. Instead, we see a new breed of Christians, softened by compromise, stripped of conviction, and lacking any real power. We have hit a spiritual wall, and something has got to change. The time has come to make a decision: What kind of Church will we be? What kind of Christian will you be? Accepted or anointed? Entertained or endued with power from on high?

What did the first-century Church have that we don't? One thing: a living revelation of Jesus Christ. And such a revelation can only come through the Holy Spirit—the Revealer Himself.

In John 14:16, Jesus makes a profound promise: "And I will pray the Father, and he shall give you another Comforter, that he may abide with you forever" (KJV). The word translated as *comforter* is *parakletos*, meaning one who comes alongside to help, guide, and empower. Interestingly, the English word *comforter* traces back to Wycliffe's translation, derived from the Latin word fortis, meaning "brave or strong." In Wycliffe's day, a comforter wasn't someone who merely consoled; it was someone who imparted strength and courage.

Why would Jesus promise a supernatural Comforter? Because following Him isn't meant to be comfortable! He asks us to do things that defy human logic and stretch us beyond our natural capacity. Jesus Himself constantly made people uneasy, whether by spitting in mud to heal blind eyes or overturning the moneychangers' tables. The gifts of the Spirit continue that same disruptive, world-altering ministry. The gifts of the Spirit are the result of the Holy Spirit revealing Jesus to us.

The apostle Paul commands believers in 1 Corinthians 14:1: "Follow after charity, and desire spiritual gifts..." (KJV). The word *desire* here means "to covet earnestly or to pursue zealously." This isn't a casual suggestion—it's a divine mandate. When teaching on this subject, I often ask people: Are you zealously seeking the gifts of the Spirit, or are you in rebellion against this clear command? Many avoid the subject because it challenges their comfort zone or because they feel unqualified to operate in the supernatural. But the gifts of the Spirit were never meant for an elite few; they are for every believer willing to step out in faith.

This is why this book by Norvel Hayes remains a timeless classic. In this book, Brother Norvel breaks down the gifts of the Spirit and their operation with clarity and simplicity, making them accessible to every believer. This book itself stands as a sign of the times. When a former Southern Baptist businessman writes such a powerful work on the gifts of the Spirit, you know God is stirring something in His Church!

Norvel Hayes didn't begin his journey aiming to write books or preach sermons, much less reach the world. He was a successful businessman who just wanted to be a "nice" little Christian who showed up on Sundays and gave offerings. But when he encountered the Holy Spirit, everything changed. What began as a personal quest to know God more deeply turned into a worldwide ministry that impacted countless lives. Brother Norvel didn't just talk about the power of God—he demonstrated it.

I had the honor of knowing him personally and witnessing the lives transformed by the extraordinary miracles in his ministry. He taught only what he had experienced and proven true through his own life and ministry. What you have in your hands is a proven manual for operating in these gifts, and there's not another one like it.

In *Activating the Nine Gifts of the Spirit*, Norvel Hayes delivers practical, actionable wisdom drawn from decades of walking with the Spirit, all conveyed in the straightforward and, at times, comical style that defined his ministry. He doesn't merely invite readers to learn about the gifts; he challenges them to step into a life where these gifts become an everyday reality. Hayes understood a vital truth that modern Christianity must reclaim: The gifts of the Spirit are not optional.

In an increasingly hostile world, believers need more than polished sermons and good intentions—we need power. Power to bring healing to the broken, deliverance to the oppressed, and hope to the hopeless.

Whether you are a seasoned believer or someone just beginning to explore the supernatural, this book will stir a hunger in you for more of God's presence. Let it be a catalyst that moves you beyond passive faith into a life marked by boldness, power, and the tangible operation of the Holy Spirit. The gifts of the Spirit are divine, unstoppable weapons, and God has opened this armory to every one of us.

Norvel Hayes lived it, taught it, and left a legacy for us to follow. Now it's your turn. The fire of the Spirit is being rekindled in these last days—step into it and be endued with power.

Alan DiDio
Pastor, The Encounter Charlotte
Host, *Encounter Today*

Chapter 1

Revival

In 1971, at a time when rioting on university campuses across America was prevalent, the Spirit of the Lord told me to go to Howard University in Washington, D.C. The students at this university had gathered all the chairs out of the dormitories and carried them downstairs to the front gate where they stacked them so nobody could get onto the campus.

Nevertheless, the Lord told me to go there, so I went. I'd been working with students on college campuses for years, so I caught a plane from Chattanooga, Tennessee, to Washington, D.C. From the airport, I took a cab to the administration building at Howard University.

Carrying my luggage, I went in and talked to the receptionist. "My name is Norvel Hayes," I said. "I'm from Tennessee. Do you have a chaplain? God told me to come here."

"Yes. Let me get Reverend Short for you," she said and returned with the chaplain at her side.

"My name is Norvel Hayes," I said. "God told me to come here."

He looked at me and said, "I believe it! Where are you staying?"

I answered, "I just got out of a cab from the airport. I'll get a motel here somewhere."

"No, we'll get you a place to stay," he said. "I believe the Lord sent you here." Then he asked if I would like to stay in a home with five Catholic priests.

"Why not?" I said. I figured it would be a good experience.

When Reverend Short took me to the home, he told me, "You're welcome to stay as long as you want. The reason they have an empty bed is that one of their priests just died in it."

"Well, I'm not going to die in it, praise God forever!" I said. "I came here on a mission. What the mission is, I don't know."

Pat Boone was supposed to speak for the chapel service in two or three days, but something happened and Pat couldn't come. The university staff called me and asked me if I'd speak in his place. I said, "Sure, if you want me to."

They told me what time the service was. I went over to the chapel hall which was totally packed. There were hundreds and hundreds of students. I sat on the stage of the auditorium with two black ministers. They invited a young man to sing a solo before they introduced me. As he was singing the solo, the Spirit of God came upon me, and I began to weep.

While I wept, I received a vision from God where I saw four winds coming down out of heaven from way up in the heavenlies somewhere. I didn't even know that God had four winds. One came from the east, one from the west, one from the north, and one from the south. All four winds came from different directions out of the heavens.

It was like four whirlwinds, and God let me see it. The four winds came together up in the heavenlies with a force and hit head-on.

There is something about the wind that God just works through, and the Spirit of God is coming like that wind. You don't know where it comes from, but it is there. The wind starts going, but where does it come from? It is like a mystery.

> **But we speak the wisdom of God in a mystery, even the hidden wisdom, which God ordained before the world unto our glory.**

> **1 Corinthians 2:7**

As the four winds became one great whirlwind, they fell to earth. And the word of the Lord came unto me saying, "This is the way the revival will come to the earth—like the wind, all of a sudden, out of heaven. Nobody will see it. It will just come. I am going to use young people as a big part to spark the revival. I will use young people to start it."

After He said this to me, I sat there still weeping. As the soloist continued to sing, the word of the Lord came unto me again saying, "When he gets through singing, stand. Go to the microphone and prophesy what you've just seen and what you've just heard. Son, prophesy what you've seen and what you've heard."

When the singer finished the song, I got out of my seat, half stumbling and half weeping, and took the microphone. The audience, very attentive, listened closely. I opened up my mouth and began to prophesy what I saw coming down from heaven. I prophesied about the four winds bringing revival to the earth and how God would use young people. I prophesied exactly what I saw and what the Lord had said to me. As I prophesied, it felt like I took a bath inside. I spoke the prophecy out in the Howard University chapel service, and the people broke out rejoicing. They were jubilant! Many of them stood weeping and rejoicing.

The next morning, I was eating breakfast in the Howard University campus cafeteria. Reverend Short saw me and came over to sit at my table. I'll never forget it as long as I live.

He said, "Mr. Hayes, the Lord has sent you here. The Lord has sent you to this university."

"Yes, I know He did," I said.

He said, "The university executives had a special meeting this morning. They were so moved by the prophecy you gave yesterday they decided to give a couple of Christian boys on campus some money to have meetings on campus to try and stop the rioting and get the students quieted down. They know that God sent you here to give that prophecy out. They believe with this kind of atmosphere, and because of the way the students responded to you when you spoke to them, that God is the answer to bringing peace to this university. We want you to have some more meetings about God."

Then he said, "God absolutely sent you here to give that prophecy out."

I said, "Oh, I believe that. I believe it now. When I came here, I didn't know what I came for, but God knew."

That was in 1971. I told that prophecy in my teaching for 14 years. Sometimes I told that story, and sometimes I told the people, "You might as well look out—there's a revival coming! You might as well look out because I've already seen it. It's coming, and God is going to use young people to start it and get it sparked."

Then in March 1985, I went to the Word of Faith Church in Dallas, Texas, to hold a satellite seminar that was supposed to last only four nights. But God had other plans.

First a boy, about 14 years old, received a vision from the Lord. A light came down from heaven and engulfed the Word of Faith Church. The boy saw angels, and he saw what God was going to do.

The next night Valarie Owen, a teacher from Word of Faith Bible School, stood and told of being caught up in the Spirit that morning:

**There was a powerful anointing, while we were praising God.
I got on my knees, then went into a trance. I could not move.**

God said these words to my heart: "Azusa Street, Azusa Street. You were interceding and breaking powers, and I'm going to pour out My Spirit as I poured out my Spirit on Azusa Street. But you haven't seen anything yet."

Azusa Street was a church in California where God began to pour out His Spirit, just like at Pentecost. God showed me this group of people were dedicated and determined to get more and more of God. They were hungry. So they got together, and they demanded from the Lord. They pulled down power from on high because they believed God. And they stayed until the power came. They say it came like a mighty rushing wind, just like on the day of Pentecost. When it fell, the people that didn't want it ran. By the time we finish, it will be Azusa Street all over again. Glory to God! Hallelujah!

The next day little third and fourth graders asked their teachers if they could pray instead of going to recess. They wanted to come down in front of the church and pray. So they came down and started praying, and the whole bunch of them fell out in the Spirit. They just fell out on the floor while they were praying, and kept on praying. They were there for two or three hours. Little kids.

The Lord had told me 14 years before that He would use little kids to spark off the revival. I was sitting on the platform when these testimonies came forth. The Holy Spirit allowed me to relive the prophecy and the vision I'd seen in Washington, D.C., in 1971. He said, "It's coming to pass. This is it. What I told you would happen is happening right before your eyes."

That night I told the people about that vision. All kinds of things started happening, both in the service and outside. People saw signs and wonders from God. They saw visions and fell out and prayed. The phone lines were jammed with testimonies of what God was doing across the country. It was the beginning of the revival that would sweep the earth.

Chapter 2

Hungry to Receive from God

B ill Kaiser, director of the Bible School at Word of Faith in Dallas, Texas, explained how a heart hungry for God sparked the Azusa Street revival.

> Toward the close of the 1900s, God found a group of hungry-hearted Bible college students in Topeka, Kansas. Charles Parham was the director. He had to leave for three days to preach a New Year's meeting in Kansas City and told his students to research the Word of God concerning the Holy Spirit while he was gone.

> Brother Parham returned on New Year's Day of 1901. His students came together and told him what they had found. They saw that every time the Holy Spirit was poured out, the initial evidence was the gift of tongues. One young student seemed to be hungrier than the rest. Her name was Agnes Osman. She quickly stepped forward and said, "Lay hands on me that I might receive the Holy Spirit and the gift of tongues."

Brother Parham was reluctant to do so, because he had never prayed for anyone to have this experience before. She pressed him. She insisted. She had enough hunger to press in.

Finally, Brother Parham laid hands on her. God honored that prayer of faith. She began to speak in a language that she had never studied, experienced, or heard before. She received the gift of tongues.

For two days nothing happened. On the third day, twelve more students received the gift of tongues. Word soon spread. Reporters came. One rabbi came to the school and listened to Sister Osman. He said, "That's a miracle. That's the most precious expression of the 23rd Psalm I have ever heard in my native Hebrew." This young lady had never studied Hebrew.

The Bible college lost the lease on their building. Charles Parham ministered around Kansas for a time. Later, he went to Houston, Texas, where he started another Bible college in 1905. There he met William Seymour, a precious Holiness preacher. Brother Seymour received the gift of tongues. He was destined to preach the Azusa Street revival.

A visiting lady pastor invited Brother Seymour to be her associate pastor in California. He went and preached his first sermon on the miracle of Pentecost and the gift of tongues. The congregation rejected him, and he couldn't stay. But he didn't let that stop him. He began to share in his own home. More and more people came. Finally, he had to stand on the front porch and preach to the people out on the lawn, because the house wasn't big enough. People began to receive the gift of tongues.

They had to find more space, so they searched and found a place at 312 Azusa Street. It was a half burned-out building that had first been a Methodist church, then a lumber yard. After the lumber yard burned down, the building was abandoned. That's the humble place where they started meeting.

They didn't have pews, so they sat on nail kegs. They didn't have a pulpit. But this precious William Seymour would kneel and pray, and the glory would fall. People got healed and delivered. For three years, three times a day, seven days a week, they had revival at Azusa Street. It all started with a hungry heart. Hallelujah, and Azusa Street lives on today!

Revival is hunger for God. You've got to get hungry. Get so hungry for revival to hit your church that you pray and cry out to God until He sends it. Don't give up. He'll send it.

Let the Holy Spirit Have His Way

As soon as we figure out who we're serving and realize who we are in Him, we can have revival all the time.

When God wants to have revival, let Him have it. God has started a lot of revivals in churches, and they just closed it down. The next time you feel the Holy Spirit start a revival spirit burning down in your bones, don't close it down. Keep on going, preach like a house on fire. Let the Spirit of God work.

Be willing to obey the Spirit. When God speaks to you, be willing to go ahead and flow with it. It's fine to have some kind of basic outline of what you might do in your service, but with the Holy Ghost, you will often wind up not following even a basic plan.

Put the Holy Ghost in charge. If you're a pastor, don't worry about your service and how you're going to run it. If the Holy Ghost is in charge, you'll know the moves to make and when to make them. You'll know that you know that you know. Let the Spirit of God be God. If He wants to heal people during a song, let Him work.

The main thing to do is to find out what the Spirit of God wants done. The Holy Spirit is heaven's representative on the earth. Decisions made by God and Jesus are always worked out on the earth by the Holy Spirit. After He gets the information from heaven about what they want done, He has another job—getting the plan over to you!

His success depends upon the condition of your human spirit. If you haven't been praying, and you don't recognize what the Holy Spirit is trying to do, you will never pick it up. And the Holy Spirit will never, never shove anything from heaven down your throat. You have to pick it up and then believe it. The price for everything from heaven has already been paid. It's all free, but it's all precious and all to be respected—everything. If you don't have a high regard and a high respect for the gifts of the Spirit, you'll never get them. God will see to it that you'll never get them.

Be sensitive to the Spirit. Some of the greatest healing services I've ever had were ones where nobody sang a song, nobody did anything. We were just quiet. But my hands were heavily anointed. The Lord would say to me, "Tonight, I want to operate. I want to perform surgery. Don't let other people say a word."

At other times, the people might sing songs and play instruments just like in an old-time Pentecostal healing meeting. It's the same thing in any of Jesus' churches. You have to learn how to be led by the Spirit of God. Worship and prayer get you close to God, and the closer you are to Him the better you can be led.

In 1965, Jesus walked into Brother Kenneth E. Hagin's room, sat down in a chair, and talked to him for an hour and a half. He talked about the gifts of the Spirit and about the Church. Jesus said, "Most of what you call full gospel churches don't have anything left except tongues and interpretation of tongues. They're growing cold." Jesus let Brother Hagin know, "I don't like it. I'm going to raise up people who will glorify the Church, glorify God, and glorify heaven."

Jesus says, "If the Son therefore shall make you free, ye shall be free indeed" (John 8:36). We need to be free from planned denominational services. Just let the Spirit of God do what He wants to do and bless people all over the world like He wants to bless them.

Revival Brings Power to the Church

The winds of revival hit with full force during the Dallas seminar in 1985, creating a giant wave of healings, miracles, and salvations. Because of satellite television, millions of people of all denominations were caught up in the revival spirit. Churches around the world reported marked increases in attendance. The revival fire hit and was spreading fast.

There are three main things to look for in a revival. First, the Church is lifted up, cleansed from sin, and restored. It takes its rightful place of importance. Second, sinners are drawn in and saved by the power of the Holy Spirit. And third, Jesus, once again, becomes the main love in the life of every believer.

Revival will bless the Church and restore it back to its rightful position. For many decades it's been only a place where people go on Sunday. The Church has lost some of its power, but revival puts power back in the Church. A church building should be a house of prayer, a house of victory, a house of love, and a house of restoration.

Many times you see a beautiful building sitting on the corner calling itself a church. You hear people say, "I go to church there. I'm Methodist." Or, "I go to church here. I'm Baptist," and so forth. "I go there every Sunday morning."

Yet, the Church is not in its rightful place like that. I want to see the Church revived and restored back in its rightful place. Then Jesus will have a chance to be Himself, save, and set people free. The Bible says, "If the Son therefore shall make you free, ye shall be free indeed" (John 8:36).

God says his "house shall be called an house of prayer" (Is. 56:7). People can go to a powerful, Jesus-filled church, pray, and make contact with God.

God's house must be a house of prayer. The heartfelt fervent prayer of a righteous man makes contact with God (Jas. 5:16). This place of prayer is where victory is found. It's where peace, salvation, healings, and miracles are found. When you make contact with God, bad nerves disappear. People find peace for their minds—peace that passes all understanding—when they make contact with God (Phil. 4:7). Revival and the spirit of prayer go hand in hand. The spirit of prayer comes out of your belly with a burning power. It changes things.

When peace comes and continues inside of you, then you know you've prayed through. Pray until you know that you know. Pray until you get victory!

The revived church is a house of victory. It's where you go to hear the Word of God in teaching, preaching, and song. God wants to make people strong by building a foundation based on the knowledge of Christ in them. People must know who they are in Christ.

In a church full of power there should be strong fellowship to teach you to live with and to love one another. A New Testament church should be filled with love and filled with the presence of God. If the right kind of atmosphere exists, people will want to go there.

And God's house should be like a hospital. All the fruit of the Spirit and the gifts of the Spirit should be in operation, restoring those who are lost and healing those who are hurt.

Security in Jesus

The most important thing to come out of revival is for people to find security in Jesus and in His Church. Then people's lives become productive and strong. The works of the devil are unraveled in a praying, revived church. The devil can't stand a praying church. He knows his work is stopped.

A true revival in God causes the whole Church to respond to righteousness, not just an arm of the Church. This revival is international in scale—Baptists, Methodists, and Pentecostals are touched by God. He's in the healing, saving, and delivering business for everyone.

For example, a black woman was called out of the audience during the Word of Faith satellite conference. She was a Baptist woman who loved Jesus. I came down to her, laid my hands on her, and said, "You foul spirit of blindness, in Jesus' name, come out of her!" At that moment she fell back on the floor and lay there weeping. When she got up, her eyes were normal. She walked on stage and said, "I can see, I can see!" These are the kinds of things that happen during revival.

The New Waves Bring What Is Lacking

There is some truth about certain kinds of ministries and certain kinds of blessings coming in waves. And if you'll notice, they usually last about one decade.

In the late 1940s, a wave of healing glory came over America and healing ministries started. God had several healing evangelists; the healing wave was strong. That lasted about 10 to 12 years.

Then there was a time when a great emphasis was put on the baptism of the Holy Spirit. The Full Gospel Business Men's Fellowship meetings were a powerful tool used by God to get denominational people baptized in the Holy Spirit. Of course, that's still going on, but there was a great wave of it for about 15 years.

I was an international director of Full Gospel Business Men's Fellowship for several years. I remember when 30 or 40 directors would be in the altar room praying and working with people, getting them baptized in the Holy Spirit. This would go on every night until midnight during entire conventions.

Next the Word people came along with a great wave of teaching. When I was growing up, nobody had much respect for the Bible teacher. That was a great shame, because it's one of the offices of the Church (1 Cor. 12:28). You learn from the teacher. That's the reason God set the office of teacher as one of the five offices of the Church. That's one of the reasons this revival kicked off the way it did. I'm a teacher, and I was teaching on the gifts of the Spirit. The teaching ministry lasted 10 to 20 years and is still flourishing.

Some people say the faith movement has waned, but God would never stop working through faith because God is a faith God. Hebrews 11:6 says, "Without faith it is impossible to please him [God]." God doesn't work if faith is not shown. He'll never get tired of faith.

All of these waves are still going on. When God sends a wave of revival across this country or around the world, I don't think it ever dies. But it does seem that He'll do something for 10 or 12 years, then He'll start doing something else really strong.

If you'll notice, the new waves supply what is being left out of the Church. God is so merciful. He doesn't want any lack in the Church. For example, the late 1950s and early 1960s brought a great surge of tongues because it had been left out. A few Pentecostals had it, but basically the Church body had been without it.

This newest wave is bringing back the miracles and healings of the New Testament Church. I believe this revival is ushering in great financial blessings to the Church on a scale we've never seen before. It is thrusting us into New Testament miracles. Prepare your heart, yield to the spirit of prayer, and see God's power come into your life in a revived fashion. God's power is available every day to everyone. You don't have to be a preacher or revivalist to get God to move for you. All you need is a repentant heart and a hunger for God.

How to Get Revival

Revival comes as a result of prayer and repentance. Pray until God comes, then weep over your sins. Tell God all about them. Ask Him to cleanse you and restore you. Pray that God will cleanse your heart and rid you of worldliness. You'll know you're home when you feel the convicting power of the Holy Ghost begin to work. Once the Church is cleansed, then the sinners can be brought in.

When you are seeking God, remember to ask for a revival for your city as well as for your church. Without one, your city will go to hell. Unless you have a vision of people going to hell, you won't do anything to rescue them. Start praying individually and corporately for a city-wide revival in all the churches. When the Holy Spirit comes—and He will come—let revival blow like the wind.

Revival begins with hunger. The hunger brings the power.

Lord, let people who read this book hunger for revival—hunger for God to visit their churches, visit their homes, and heal their little children as they sleep in their beds. Let people be hungry for God every day, not just on Sunday. Let them get hungry for heaven. Let them get hungry for pure love that's real. Let them get hungry for Jesus. In Jesus' name. Amen.

Why Have Revival?

Revival makes a church red hot and aflame with the Spirit. Some people believe the way they want to believe, instead of believing what Matthew, Mark, Luke, and John say. Then when death comes knocking on their door, they'd like to flow really quick to where the blessing is. It's not that easy.

If you want Jesus to be the Jesus of the New Testament, you can't go to a cold church and get it. You have to go somewhere where the Word of God is being preached, taught, and expounded upon.

If you aren't going to a church that expounds upon Jesus as your Healer, you probably won't get healed. Jesus has to hear something. Faith has a voice.

In the Church of the Lord Jesus Christ (the New Testament Church), an altar is a sacred thing. An altar is a place of prayer, repentance, and worship. Weeping all that junk out of you around the altar brings God on the scene. An altar is holy, clean, sacred, and true. You can see in the Old and New Testaments that God, Jesus, and the Holy

Spirit all love the altar. They love an altar in a church where people can come before God in Jesus' name. The altar represents Him. When you come to meet Him, He meets you because Jesus is the Head of the Church, and He loves His Church.

An altar is in your heart, too. You can stop and pray anywhere, anytime. Close your eyes, shut out the world, and enter into the presence of the living God. If you don't know Jesus, pray the prayer below, and pray it loudly. Speak it boldly, but humbly.

Oh, Lord God, I come to Your throne in Jesus' name. As a sinner—someone lost and without hope in this world—I ask You to come and be my Lord (Rom. 10:9–10). Break up the foundations of sin in my life. Cleanse me and seal me for eternity with Your sweet Spirit. Baptize me in Your Holy Spirit (Acts 2).

Oh, God, forgive my sins. They are as scarlet. But You can make them white as snow (Is. 1:18). I lay my sins on the altar now. Send down Your fire and consume them, oh, God (Heb. 12:29).

Teach me, like a little child, to lift my eyes toward heaven and call You my Father. Be my Healer, keep me revived and hungry for You. With an uplifted voice I thank You, Father, for saving my soul and healing my body. You are mine and I am yours. In Jesus' name. Amen.

You will never know what life is all about until you make contact with Jesus. Even though you may be a rich man, you will never know what royalty is about until you meet Him. His sweet presence is like royalty flowing through your veins, flowing through your bones. It makes life worth living, just to have the Holy Spirit inside you. Accepting Jesus is like being adopted into the royal family, the highest family in the world. You feel like you're rich from the top of your head to the bottom of your feet. What you have in your pocketbook has nothing to do with it. You can live in royalty on the inside of you.

It is God's will for His people to prosper, but having His Spirit flowing through you is sweet! You're a member of the royal family.

Let the revival fire burn inside of you. Hunger for God. Let the Holy Spirit's presence make your life sweet.

Chapter 3

Gifts of the Holy Spirit

Now concerning spiritual gifts, brethren, I would not have you ignorant . . . . But the manifestation of the Spirit is given to every man to profit withal.

For to one is given by the Spirit the word of wisdom; to another the word of knowledge by the same Spirit;

To another faith by the same Spirit; to another the gifts of healing by the same Spirit;

To another the working of miracles; to another prophecy; to another discerning of spirits; to another divers kinds of tongues; to another the interpretation of tongues:

But all these worketh that one and the selfsame

Spirit, dividing to every man severally as he will.

1 Corinthians 12:1, 7–11

The nine gifts of the Spirit come in three categories: power gifts, revelation gifts, and vocal gifts. The power gifts are faith, miracles, and healing; the revelation gifts are word of knowledge, word of wisdom, and discerning of spirits; and the vocal gifts are prophecy, tongues, and interpretation of tongues.

The gift of faith is a gift of power where God's power explodes and comes on you and changes you into what God needs you to be at that moment. The gift of healing is God's healing power that comes into manifestation all of a sudden. The third power gift is the working of miracles.

There are three revelation gifts. The word of wisdom points toward the future. The word of knowledge supernaturally shows you things about the present. It's a manifestation of the Spirit where God shows you the condition of things in your house or your business or somebody's life He wants you to help. The other revelation gift is the discerning of spirits. The Holy Spirit will manifest Himself and show you things in the spirit realm. God will show you things He doesn't want you involved in or show you spirits that are not of God.

The vocal gifts are prophecy, tongues, and interpretation. Prophecy is when God's power comes to you and the Holy Spirit manifests Himself on the inside of you. The ministry gift boils up supernaturally with words in a known language (words that you know) that God wants you to speak out. With tongues, the Spirit of God will manifest Himself in a supernatural unknown language (words you don't know) that flow out of you. Then God's power will come on another person in manifestation and give him or her the interpretation in English of what you said in tongues.

These nine gifts of the Spirit are very important to the Church today. They are the weapons of our warfare. A church that is trying to fight a spiritual battle without the gifts of the Spirit will never win. The devil will rob them of the very thing God wants them to have simply because they don't know anything about the gifts of the Spirit.

The Holy Spirit is stronger than the devil, and the gifts of the Spirit provide the power to overcome the devil.

You might say, "Do you mean the Lord wants me to speak in tongues in a church service?" Not necessarily. The gift of tongues is a calling, a tool for public ministry. You may never do that, but God does want you to speak in tongues, to pray in the Spirit.

Praying in the Spirit or praying in tongues is the most powerful way to pray. God doesn't want us ignorant when it comes to praying and speaking in tongues.

You may say, "Well, my church doesn't believe in that." It doesn't make any difference what your church believes or even what I say; it's what the Bible says that counts. The Bible is for all churches.

God changes not. He is not going to throw out 1 Corinthians 12 just because you don't believe in it; it's going to operate for those who believe it. The gifts of the Spirit will operate through those who are available.

The Gifts Are Weapons

The gifts are given to profit withal—every man, every woman, everybody who belongs to God's Church. The gifts come down from heaven and are called *weapons*.

For the weapons of our warfare are not carnal, but mighty through God to the pulling down of strong holds.

2 Corinthians 10:4

You're in a battle. You say, "What do you mean I'm in a battle? The battle has already been won. It's already been won by Jesus." But you're not Jesus. Is that clear?

The battle has already been won by Jesus. The price has already been paid. On the cross, the price has already been paid by the stripes on His back for your healing. He's already been to hell. He's already taken the keys away from the devil.

Keys

Jesus got a set of keys to give you.

Jesus said of the Church He built, "The gates of hell shall not prevail against it" (Matt. 16:18). But the Church needs the gifts of the Spirit operating. The Church needs God's weapons operating to let you put a stop to what the devil is trying to do to you.

The gifts give you power by faith to do anything: healing, miracles, tongues and interpretation to build you up, and prophecy to build the whole Church up.

Jesus said, "When you get born again by the Spirit of God and become part of the Church, I'll give you a set of keys, believer."

That's all you're ever going to get on this earth. That's all. You inherited heaven when you got born again. But this is the thing that the Lord Jesus Christ wants you to understand: you're not in heaven yet. You're living here on earth. You have to work every day, and you have to fight devils.

Jesus said, "I will give unto thee the keys of the kingdom of heaven" (Matt. 16:19). There are a lot of things in the kingdom of heaven. But that's no sign that you'll ever get them. It all depends on if you find the right key or not.

There is one key on the great key ring of God that says divine healing. That's no sign that you'll ever be healed, though. It all depends on if you take the time to dig into God's Word and find the key to healing. Even after you find it, you have to pull it out of the Word and stick the key into heaven by faith. You have to turn it yourself or put action to your faith. When you do, healing flows down to you.

There is a key on God's key ring that says financial success. Most people never find it. There is a key on there that says spiritual success where God takes you into the things of the Spirit.

God wants the things of the Spirit to go forth. There are all kinds of good things in the set of keys that Jesus gives to the believer. But if you're not a student of the Scriptures, you'll never find the keys. That's the sad part. If you don't study the Scriptures, and don't take time to dig and read, you won't ever get a hold of the keys that belong to you and that you need.

Things from heaven—promises in the New Testament—fall on you because you believe the Bible, and your faith pulls them out of heaven down to you on earth.

It's not fair for sick people to walk into a church and go home sick. You need to have the ministry of the laying on of hands. Then I'll guarantee you that God's healing power will flow from your hands into the sick person.

Go out to the byways and to your neighbors, and lay hands on them in Jesus' name. Watch the healing power of God go into them. Some of them will accept it, and some won't. But that won't have anything to do with it. It will come through you.

Jesus has given you the keys. Read the Bible for yourself and find out what's in there. Memorize what you get from God. Know and memorize 1 Corinthians 12. If you'll get that chapter in you, it will be just like anything else. When you need something, the Holy Spirit will come and manifest Himself to help you. I don't care if it's the gift of faith, the gift of the working of miracles, or what gift it is. He'll come as the Spirit wills. You can't make God do anything.

The Gifts Operate to Profit Humanity

God does things through the Holy Ghost as He wills. It's something that God does. You can't make the healing power of God come upon you. But if you just talk about it, it will come because the Lord says, "I'll go with you and confirm the Word with signs following."

27

You can't make the healing power of God come upon you, but if God has given it to you (and your ministry is a gift), it will always come whenever you teach on it. But sometimes it will be ten times stronger than at other times.

To get your mind straightened out so you can see the whole body of Christ needs every one of the gifts, read verse 18 closely: "But now hath God set the members every one of them in the body."

God has sent all of the nine gifts of the Spirit to be given to the Church by the Holy Ghost. The last part of that verse says "as it hath pleased him." It pleased Him to give the gift of the word of knowledge to Kathryn Kuhlman. It pleased Him to give me the gift of working of miracles to get people new hearts. The gifts operate to profit humanity. God chooses the ministry gift and, by His will, decides what gift will operate.

I don't know why He chooses certain people. It is as He wills, not as you or I will. Sometimes God sends me a thousand miles to bring one message in tongues at some convention somewhere.

Why does He do that? I have no earthly idea. There are probably 500 people there who could speak in tongues—I have no earthly idea why He would send me. But sometimes He does. This is one of the gifts God has given me to minister in public.

> **But now hath God set the members every one of them in the body, as it hath pleased him. And if they were all one member where were the body? But now are they many members, yet but one body. And the eye cannot say unto the hand, I have no need of thee: nor again the head to the feet, I have no need of you.**
>
> **1 Corinthians 12:18–21**

This means you need all nine gifts in manifestation, not just one. Don't get lopsided. Seek all the gifts.

Wherefore I give you to understand, that no man speaking by the Spirit of God calleth Jesus accursed: and that no man can say that Jesus is the Lord, but by the Holy Ghost.

Now there are diversities of gifts, but the same Spirit. And there are differences of administrations, but the same Lord. And there are diversities of operations, but it is the same God which worketh all in all. But the manifestation of the Spirit is given to every man to profit withal.

1 Corinthians 12:3-7

Some people say, "Brother Norvel, it might not be God's will for me to have that or the Lord might not want to do that for me." He wants to do it for you where it's preached, believed, and expounded upon. He wants to do it, but if He never hears your faith in 1 Corinthians 12, He never performs it for you. All of the nine gifts are free. He wants to give them to you as gifts. That's why they're called gifts.

"But the manifestation of the Spirit is given to every man to profit withal" (v.7). That means to profit with all heaven has. Glory to God! The gifts are given to every man; He'll give them to you. Keep all the doubt out of you, and don't ever say again, "Maybe God doesn't want me to have a miracle or a healing." Yes, He does. It's been provided for you.

You might say, "Well, the gifts of the Spirit don't work for everybody." That's not what the Bible says.

Now there are times when God will manifest a gift powerfully through an individual for public ministry. I used to work in large conventions with Kathryn Kuhlman. She gave me a special pass to come to her meetings anytime I wanted. Sister Kuhlman was a woman who found favor with God. He gave her two strong gifts—the word of knowledge and the gifts of healing. These gifts were very strong in her ministry. She also had the gift of working of miracles operating in her services. Her whole ministry was built on these gifts, and she protected them by not allowing anything to come between her and the Holy Spirit.

That's probably why the gifts operated so strongly; she protected them with her life! She called down immediately anybody who tried to interfere with them. In every service the gifts would flow. Hundreds of people were healed and saved. Sinners sat and watched her services for hours. Lots of times they would get healed in the overflow. I've been to services of hers that lasted five or six hours because the Holy Ghost would start working. It was something else.

But the same word of knowledge that Kathryn Kuhlman had to minister in public, you can have yourself on a lesser scale as you need it. It's available for you. God didn't write the Bible for some people and not for others. God didn't give nine gifts of the Spirit to the Church for just some people. But He does choose some people to minister those things in public under a special anointing.

God has called me and given me a particular gift of working of miracles to operate in my ministry; people receive new hearts from God. You could come forward and not get one if you boldly just wouldn't believe God. But probably 95 percent of the people who come forward to get a new heart, get one. That started operating in my ministry in 1971. I was in the back seat of a car in Carbondale, Illinois, on my way to a meeting, and God gave me that gift of healing.

Sometimes my heart will begin to hurt, and it will hurt for an hour or two. It will hurt so badly I'll have to lay my hand over my heart. The Lord will say, "You'd better obey me tonight." I'll call people down for new hearts, and He just pumps new hearts into their chests.

You Need All the Gifts of the Spirit

You can't say, "I've got healing. I don't need miracles." Or, "I've got miracles, I don't need prophecy." Or, "I've got wisdom, I don't need tongues and interpretation."

For as the body is one, and hath many members, and all the members of that one body, being many are one body: so also is Christ . . . . But now hath God set the members every one of them in the body, as it hath pleased him. And if they were all one member, where were the body? But now are they many members, yet but one body. And the eye cannot say unto the hand, I have no need of thee: nor again the head to the feet, I have no need of you.

1 Corinthians 12:18–21

God says you're going to need every one of them. There's coming a time in your life when you'll need every one of the gifts of the Spirit because they are God's weapons to fight the devil. They are God's power. That's the sum and substance of the gifts of the Spirit.

Channels for God's Power

All of us are channels for the power of God to work through. The Spirit of God rescued each of us from sin. I was in sin just like you were before the Spirit of God visited my life.

Before your spirit was reborn, you might have been a drunkard, an adulterer, a thief, or a liar. It really doesn't matter what you were or what you've done in the past. You've been forgiven. God has taken all of your sins, pulled them out of you, and threw them into the depths of the sea of forgetfulness. He has blocked them from His memory. The only ones remembering them are you and the devil.

Don't let the devil tell you that you're not worthy. That's a lie! God wants to use you. If you are saved or born again, you stand before God as white as snow today as a candidate for the gifts of the Spirit. So make your mind, your body, and your spirit available for these gifts to operate through as the Spirit wills to use you.

Chapter 4

Getting in Shape to Receive

"How can I get myself in shape to receive the gifts of the Spirit?" you ask. There's only one way. You have to be delivered from yourself. How do you do that? By the fire of God.

Remember on the day of Pentecost when God sent fire into the Upper Room with His Spirit? The fire of God follows God's Spirit. And what does fire do? It burns. The fire of God burns, demolishes, does away with, and makes things disappear that don't need to be there. There are so many Full Gospel people who should know better but don't know very much about the fire of God. The fire of God is so important to get a person delivered, to burn the chaff out.

In other words, you have to be delivered from yourself so you can receive what the Holy Ghost wants to give you. Whether you know it or not, you are your own worst enemy. You can't go by what somebody else does. You have to pray, get a hold of God, and worship God yourself.

Your mate may worship God three hours a day and pray two hours a day, but that's not going to get you any victory from heaven. You've got to do it yourself. Jesus is a personal Jesus. You can't live on your mate's experience from God. You can't live on your relatives' experiences from God. You can't live on the fact that your mother was a good Christian. You've got to bow down your knees before Almighty God yourself and make Him the living God of your life.

The Spirit world is real, and all of these beautiful gifts that God wants to give to you are weapons from God to the Church. They are weapons to do away with the works of the devil. God doesn't want His believers, His children, putting up with the devil.

You wouldn't have to put up with him if you didn't listen to him. Jesus said, "Don't listen to the devil. You can't believe anything he says. The truth is not in him" (John 8:44).

You just have to watch the devil's deceiving power. He'll try to put a partial truth over on you. It will seem so right to you. But after you've done it, you'll say, "How did I ever get into that mess?"

You didn't pray through and get the mind of God. You did it just because it seemed right at the time. The devil will give you four or five things that seem right and tell you one big lie so he can trick you. He'll get you all goofed up, messed up, weak, and confused.

But God's got weapons to let you know what's going on. So be willing to listen to the three vocal gifts: tongues, interpretations, and prophecy. When they roll out of somebody supernaturally, and the Holy Spirit witnesses to you, be willing to study the interpretation, study prophecy.

Now, why can't you receive those weapons from God? Is there some reason why you can't receive those nine gifts of the Spirit like you're supposed to receive them? Sure, there is.

For what the law could not do, in that it was weak through the flesh, God sending his own Son in the likeness of sinful flesh,

and for sin, condemned sin in the flesh: That the righteousness of the law might be fulfilled in us, who walk not after the flesh, but after the Spirit.

Romans 8:3–4

The righteousness of the law won't be fulfilled in you unless you walk after the Spirit. You have to be hungry for the Spirit.

For they that are after the flesh do mind the things of the flesh; but they that are after the Spirit the things of the Spirit. For to be carnally minded is death; but to be Spiritually minded is life and peace.

For if ye live after the flesh, ye shall die: but if ye through the Spirit do mortify the deeds of the body, ye shall live. For as many as are led by the Spirit of God, they are the sons of God.

Romans 8:5–6, 13–14

The sons and daughters of God are robbed for only one reason—not two—just one: Because they are not led by the Spirit of God.

For ye have not received the spirit of bondage again to fear; but ye have received the Spirit of adoption, whereby we cry, Abba, Father.

Romans 8:15

If you're born again, you've received the Spirit of adoption where you cry Father. You can walk around crying *Father*. "Oh, Father, healing is for me. Oh, Father, mercies are for me. Father, the gifts of the Spirit are for me. Father, a clear mind is for me. Father, financial success is for me."

But you have to say that it's for you. As long as you wonder, it won't work. God doesn't answer wondering prayers. He answers faith prayers. He answers confession prayers.

The Spirit itself beareth witness with our spirit, that we are the children of God.

Romans 8:16

Does the Spirit of God ever manifest Himself to you? That's a sign that you're a child of God.

If you and I are children of God, why don't we believe our Father? If we would only believe Him, we could receive everything He wants to give us.

He is the Father, and you are the child. The Spirit that is in you will bear witness that you are a child of God. The Bible says that your Father will not withhold one good thing from you.

It Wasn't Easy at First

You might ask, "Was it easy to yield yourself to the Spirit of God?" No, it was not. When you first begin to yield, it will usually scare you. It did me. The Lord Jesus put words in me and tried to get me to prophesy, but I'd hold on to the church pew. He'd shake me, and I'd cry. It scared me so badly.

He would boil up in me, giving me the words, but I didn't want to get up and say them out. I loved the Lord, but I was afraid I'd say something wrong. I just wouldn't do it. I mean, for two or three years I hung onto the back of the pew. But I'll tell you what. Tongues and interpretation can bring confidence to you. It can build a foundation in you.

I was in Tulsa, Oklahoma, at Brother Hagin's apartment late one Sunday afternoon. We were having a little prayer meeting. Brother and Sister Goodwin were also there. All of a sudden, Sister Goodwin came over to me and started speaking in tongues. When she got through, Brother Goodwin walked over, and this is the word that he said to me: "Now, Son, those words that I've been putting in you, I want you to get up and speak those words out. I want you to go home, and I want you to get permission from your pastor to get up in the church and speak out those words. If your pastor refuses you, I'm going to give you the ministry anyway" (but not there, in other words).

I went home and asked the pastor. I said, "Jesus said for me to come and get permission from you. When the Lord puts prophecy on me, do you want to give me permission to speak them out?"

"Oh, yes, Brother Norvel," he said. "You know you can obey God in this church. Just go ahead and obey the Lord."

"Well, we'll just have to wait and see," I said. But sure enough, it came about two weeks later on a Sunday night at the end of the service. God moved on me and melted me.

Since that tongues and interpretation from the Goodwins, I'd been thinking about what the Lord had told me. It ministered to me and gave me strength and confidence. So, I got up and spoke out the words God gave me. As soon as I got the last word out, God came on me so strong and started blessing me so much. I just fell on my knees, weeping and getting blessed. I found out God loves me, and He was petting me because I obeyed the Holy Spirit.

When God was training me, molding me, and bringing me up in the Spirit in those days, He'd bless me. I'd start reading the Bible in the morning in bed. I'd get so involved, and scriptures would start jumping out at me. The Lord would begin to shake me, and I couldn't read the Bible anymore. I'd just lie down with tears streaming down my cheeks. I felt like all my bones were going to jump out of my body.

Sometimes He would shake me from 8 o'clock until noon. My bed would shake for three or four hours. I mean my bed would shake. I couldn't even stop it. I would just be saying, "Oh, Jesus! Jesus!" Talk about getting blessed!

So, the gifts began to operate through me, because I was ministered to by a precious couple that the Holy Ghost operated through; they knew how to minister to me. The Spirit of God knew exactly what I wanted and what I needed. I needed Brother and Sister Good-win to minister to me. I needed for God to tell me, "I'm putting words in you, and son, I want you to get up and speak them out."

Chapter 5

God's Gifts Solve Problems

I believe your whole life will change if you'll listen to what the Spirit of the Lord says concerning the gifts of the Spirit. The gifts of the Holy Spirit are the answers to all of the world's problems. The gifts of the Spirit are the answers to all of *your* problems.

Always remember this: You will never have a problem in your life that the gifts of the Spirit can't correct and give you information about. They cover all of the problems that you have now or ever will have. If the United States President had all nine gifts of the Spirit operating in his life, his worries would be over because in every situation he would know what to do in advance.

Everything you need is in 1 Corinthians 12—all those beautiful gifts, given out as the Spirit wills. The Holy Spirit wills to give them out continually wherever they're taught and wherever they're believed.

The Ministry of the Holy Spirit

The only reason we don't get any more help from God than we do is because we don't know the ministry of the Holy Spirit.

The Holy Spirit would make you rich if you'd let Him. But of course, until you learn to handle money, He won't do that. He would heal you if you'd let Him. He knows exactly how to heal you. He'd give you a miracle. The Holy Spirit would create things for you if you'd show God you trust Him to that degree.

If you go to church, you trust God generally. You have a general type faith that believes God can do anything. But as long as you live, remember this: God won't accept that. God won't accept general faith. You have to be specific with God if you want the Holy Spirit to manifest Himself. As long as you walk around saying, "Well, I believe that Jesus could do anything. I believe God could do anything," the Holy Spirit, who lives in your belly, just dwells there. He'll never manifest Himself even though He has been sent from heaven to bring heaven's blessings to you.

Third John 2 says, "I wish above all things that thou mayest prosper and be in health, even as thy soul prospereth." In heaven you will see the height of wealth. In heaven they don't even know the meaning of poverty. If you'll work for God in your life, when you get to heaven, you'll probably have diamond doorknobs. There is no poverty in heaven, just like there are no diseases.

You hear people quote, "There are no diseases in heaven, there will be no cripples in heaven, there will be no blind people in heaven." That's right. But also, there will be no poverty in heaven.

The Holy Spirit, the Person who lives in your belly, thinks exactly like heaven is. He doesn't think any other way. That's where He came from. That's all He's ever known. He is consumed with positive energy creating wealth, health, and miracles. He brings good things to you. He will do anything for you, that is, anything heaven has to offer.

Jesus did a lot of good things, and when He told people He was going away, they got all shook up. But Jesus plainly explained things to them. He said, "No. Don't get shook up because it's good for you that I go away. If I go not away, the Comforter will not come. But when He comes, He will be in you. He will guide you, lead you into all truth, and teach you." The Holy Spirit is the Great Teacher. He'll teach you all truth about anything. He's the Teacher of the Church.

In every area of your life where you're not successful, you're not being led by the Spirit of God, because He thinks no other way except success. He's consumed with it. He thinks only about success.

The reason the Church per se is so crippled is because the nine gifts of the Holy Ghost are not in operation as they should be. The nine gifts of the Spirit are the answer to all the world's problems—every one of them. Every church in the world is supposed to have all nine gifts in operation allowing the Holy Spirit to give His ministry out as He wills.

The Holy Spirit has a ministry. He has gifts He wants to give you. The nine gifts of the Holy Spirit are His ministry. They are not your ministry. You can't make one gift of the Spirit operate. The gifts of the Holy Spirit are given to a believer as the Spirit wills (1 Cor. 12:11). You're the vessel it comes through.

Learn to Receive from Heaven

For you to receive from heaven is the most simple thing in the world, but you have to learn how to do it. You'll never learn with your mind. You have to pray that you'll have the mind of Christ so you can understand the Bible and accept it just the way it's written. God will do great and mighty things for you! He'll do anything for you. It is not God's will that He withhold any good thing from you. It's God's good pleasure to give you your heart's desire and so many gifts that you don't have enough room to contain them (Ps. 37:4, 84:11; Mal. 3:10).

You say, "Well, I wish I had some of them."

You can get them. I urge you to seek all nine of the gifts of the Spirit.

The Gifts Can Save Your Life

The graveyard is full of people who don't even know what's in 1 Corinthians 12. If you don't know what's in there, it can cost you your life.

One manifestation of the Holy Ghost through one gift can absolutely save your life—just one manifestation. You need to study, learn, and know what all the nine gifts are, and you need every one of them. Don't think you'll ever just need healing and miracles. You need all nine of them.

A time in your life is coming when you're going to be desperate for every one of the nine gifts of the Spirit. And every one of them you leave out—pay no respect to or don't spend time learning about—might just be the link that will be missing. It will be a blessing from Almighty God meant for you that you can't have. God won't give it to you, because every part of the New Testament that you leave out of your life, that's the part you can't have. You have to learn what's in the Bible. You have to be steadfast. You have to know that you know that you know what's in there. You have to tell God you know what's in there. If you tell God that and tell Him you believe it, He'll give it to you.

He'll manifest Himself and give it to anybody, anywhere. It doesn't make any difference to Him. God's not selfish. Don't leave a missing link in your life and limit how the Holy Spirit can use you. Learn all you can, because God works only with knowledge.

Trust God

Sometimes the Holy Spirit will rise up in me and just weep. Once, after weeping for a long time, He said to me, "Oh, son, I want to heal the sick so much. I wish they could trust Me. I wish they would believe Me. I have been sent to the earth to heal them. I've been sent to the earth to stretch their legs out. I've been sent to the earth to open up their blind eyes. I wish they would believe Me and trust Me. I wish they would praise Jesus, because He's the Healer. I'll do the work for them. I've been sent here to do the work. But they must trust Me."

It's called faith in God. It's called trust. Remember that faith trusts God. Tell people that Jesus heals, and that's it. He heals everyone who will believe in Him. Boldly tell people that God will heal them. Don't be backward, and don't be ashamed of it. Always remember, anything you're ashamed of God won't give to you. If you're ashamed of Jesus the Healer, then Jesus will be your Savior, but He'll never become your Healer. The bolder you can believe it, the better God likes it. The more heaven shouts and rejoices, the more the Holy Spirit will rise up within you and give you exactly what you want from God.

'Given to Every Man'

Look at 1 Corinthians 12:7. It will keep you free from yourself. It will keep you free from false doctrines. It will keep you free from allowing your mind to think that Jesus might not want you to have the gifts of the Spirit. It says, "But the manifestation of the Spirit is given to every man to profit withal."

Say it out loud, "Every man means me." Believe it! If you'll say that every day, and know that the Spirit has been given to manifest Himself to you personally, then you'll keep all those lies out of your mind. You'll keep all those deceiving spirits from the devil out of your mind.

Remember, the gifts will help you in your business. They'll help you in your relationships. They'll help you in anything that concerns you. One of the nine gifts of the Spirit can solve any problem you have.

Chapter 6

Teaching Is Vital

God is not lazy; He's diligent. God is not poor; He's very wealthy. God is not ignorant; He's very intelligent, and God just won't deal through ignorance. So, if you're going to get God to do anything for you, you're going to have to get smart.

Wherever I go, I suggest to pastors to hold seminars in their churches at least once a year on the gifts of the Holy Spirit. They can teach it themselves or have a visiting minister. Then, I suggest that during the year, as the Lord leads, they preach on one gift some Sunday, then another until they cover all nine.

The more you teach on it, the more you preach on it, the more you talk about it, the more you recognize it, and the more you expound upon it, the more the gifts will work for you. They will come into manifestation for you. All the nine gifts of the Spirit are given to you through the Holy Spirit as the Spirit wills, and the Spirit always wills wherever the Word is preached.

The Word and the Spirit Agree

If 1 Corinthians 12 is not preached in a given church, then the Spirit doesn't will to give the gifts of the Spirit there. The Holy Spirit is on earth only to confirm the Word with signs following. The Holy Spirit is a first-class performer. He performs the New Testament for anybody who will believe it. He has been sent by God, through a prayer that Jesus prayed, to help people, to teach people, and to perform the New Testament (John 16). The Holy Spirit will perform any verse you will believe and not doubt. He'll give it to you. You have to understand that. The Word and the Holy Spirit agree.

You may say, "Well, why doesn't the Holy Spirit do more for me?" I can answer that quickly. He doesn't agree with your head. You're too far out for Him. If you will remind God of what you believe, then quote chapter and verse, the Holy Spirit will come alive because He confirms the Word with signs following. If you will study 1 Corinthians 12 and believe all of it, He'll perform it for you. The Spirit and the Word agree.

If you're going to deal with God and the gifts of the Holy Spirit, you're going to have to believe 1 Corinthians 12. You're going to have to show respect for it. You have to think it's precious and desire and hunger for all nine gifts of the Spirit. When you do and you believe, they come easily through the Holy Ghost on the inside of you. So keep your human spirit in good enough shape to pick up what the Holy Spirit is trying to do.

When you get born again by the Spirit of God, your human spirit takes on a new nature, because Divinity Himself comes to indwell you. The channel God uses to communicate with your spirit is the Holy Spirit. You don't know what you need; you only think you do. You know what you need in some cases, but there will be times in life when you won't know how to pray. That's when the Holy Ghost will lead you and guide you into the truth (John 16).

Make up your mind to believe God can help you. Then He'll help you through the Holy Ghost by speaking to your spirit.

Study to Show Yourself Approved

Study the Word of God and show yourself approved. Show God that you believe the Bible. You can't believe it unless you study it. Any part of the Bible you show God you believe, He will give to you. You don't have to show people anything, but you have to show God.

You have to show God you believe the book of Galatians. You have to show Him you believe the book of Luke. If you don't, you can't have it. God won't give it to you. God says you have to remind Him of the scripture that you're standing on; remind Him of the words you believe (Is. 43:26.) For the rest of your life, you have to remind Him. Pick out a scripture that covers your case and remind Him.

That's the reason it's so important to begin studying, learning, and keeping your own mind renewed with the Word of God after you get born again by the Spirit of God. The Holy Spirit works only through knowledge, and you're not as smart as the Holy Spirit!

You may think you know a lot about God. But when you start getting in tune with the Holy Spirit, He'll let you know there are a lot of things about God you don't know.

Every Church Gets the Gospel They Preach

I'm sorry to say this, but most churches built on this earth are ignorant of all the gifts of the Spirit. The gifts of the Spirit are the very thing God said He did not want us ignorant of, but most churches are ignorant of them just the same.

Suppose I went out and canvassed 100 pastors from different denominations, lined them up, and tested them on where the gifts of the Spirit were found in the Bible. We'd probably lose 75 of them right then. If on my next test, I asked them to list the nine gifts of the Spirit, we'd lose 20 more of them. We would only have five left. If I then gave them 10 minutes to write the definition of each of the nine gifts of the Spirit and list how they operate, we might possibly have only two or three left.

My point is this: God works for the body through the knowledge of the pastor. You can contact God and believe for yourself, but usually you only believe what they teach where you go to church. If you're Baptist, you usually believe what the Baptists believe. If you're Methodist, you believe what they believe. If you belong to a Catholic church, then you listen to the priest. And if you go to the Church of Christ, you believe what they say.

But the truth is, we all need to study the Bible. God says, "I change not" (Mal. 3:6). He stays steadfast all the time. God is love and has always been from the Old Testament to the New Testament. Seven of the gifts of the Spirit listed in the New Testament for the Church today also operated in the Old Testament. The only two gifts of the Spirit that did not operate in the Old Testament are tongues and interpretation of tongues. They came into being after the Day of Pentecost, when tongues first visited the 120 in the upper room (Acts 2).

Get the Gifts Flowing

Pastors must remind God about the nine gifts of the Spirit: Word of wisdom, word of knowledge, gift of faith, working of miracles, gifts of healing, prophecy, divers tongues, interpretation of tongues, and discerning of spirits. Tell God you want all of them. Tell God, "I believe in all nine of them." Remind God of the book of Corinthians. If you don't do that, the gifts of the Spirit begin to wane and die and do not manifest themselves. Then you get into a religious rut.

If you are a pastor, take your Bible into the sanctuary in the afternoon when nobody's there, and open it up to 1 Corinthians 12. Lay it on the floor. Get on your knees and lean over it. Stare at it. Make up your mind that you want the nine gifts of the Spirit in your church. Start praying and claim all nine gifts of the Spirit. Walk the floor like Elisha, to and fro. Hold up the Bible and tell the Lord you want these gifts. Cry out in a loud voice, "Oh, God, I want these nine gifts of the Spirit for my people, for my congregation. They have a right, Jesus. They have accepted You, Jesus, in their lives, and they have a right to be blessed from heaven. I want all nine gifts of the Spirit to operate in this church, Jesus." (If you are not a pastor, take the same principle and get the gifts flowing.)

If you'll tell God you want the gifts, the Holy Ghost will have the freedom and right to manifest them in your church. And the Holy Ghost will start giving out His ministry through the gifts. He may call one person and lay it upon him or her to speak in tongues in public, or He may give someone the supernatural gift of knowledge.

When God hears 1 Corinthians 12, He's ready to manifest it. If you are a pastor, I'm telling you again: Teach your people on the gifts. Hold revivals. Teach seminars. If you don't, it won't be long before you begin thinking, *I've been preaching in my church for years, and God never comes down and heals anybody here. I wonder why?*

"So then faith cometh by hearing, and hearing by the word of God" (Rom. 10:17). Faith in any of God's provisions comes by hearing. When I first came into the Full Gospel movement, God told me to begin a study about faith. He said, "I'll lead you into other things later." And He did. I was faithful. I'd study and study until He unfolded His Word to me. So when I started teaching on the gifts of the Spirit, it wasn't very long until He started manifesting them.

God will do the same for you. Lay hands on the sick. If you don't feel a thing, claim it by faith. Faith praying is so important. If you don't know what faith is, you can't get much done. Some people don't get an instant manifestation. That was true even when Jesus laid hands on people (Luke 17:12–19). It is our responsibility to teach them how to receive by faith.

Faith is believing something you don't see (Heb. 11:1). Faith is not seeing. It is not touching. In John 20:29, Jesus said to Thomas (who we call Doubting Thomas), "because thou hast seen me, thou has believed: blessed are they that have not seen, and yet have believed."

That's what faith is, believing something you don't feel, touch, or see. Only believe, and you will see the glory of the Lord.

When you believe it and are listening really close, it will come. All of a sudden, right out of the clear blue sky, the Holy Spirit will fall on somebody and begin to heal them openly.

It could happen anywhere across this great country. Don't be surprised if a cripple sitting beside you just gets up and walks off. Don't be surprised if a blind person stands up and says, "I can see! I can see!" Don't be surprised if a deaf person beside you stands up and yells, "I can hear everything!" With God all things are possible (Matt. 19:26).

When the Spirit of God flows, whatever work He's doing flows and flows. Sometimes I've known God to heal sinners. At times the power will fall and get on everyone. You get the gospel you preach.

Chapter 7

The Word of Wisdom

In 1 Corinthians 12, Paul says, "For to one is given by the Spirit the word of wisdom . . . " (verse 8). What does he mean? The gift of the word of wisdom is a word from God about what will take place in the future, a divine revelation of future events.

You may say, "Why do I need the gift of the word of wisdom"? To answer that question, read 1 Corinthians 12 again and see what Paul has to say about the spiritual gifts:

> Now concerning spiritual gifts, brethren, I would not have you ignorant. Ye know that ye were Gentiles, carried away unto these dumb idols, even as ye were led.

> Wherefore I give you to understand, that no man speaking by the Spirit of God calleth Jesus accursed: and that no man can say that Jesus is the Lord, but by the Holy Ghost.

> Now there are diversities of gifts, but the same Spirit. And there are differences of administrations, but the same Lord. And there are diversities of operations, but it is the same God which worketh all in all.

> But the manifestation of the Spirit is given to every man to profit withal.

1 Corinthians 12:1–7

Each gift of the Spirit has its place. One cannot take the place of the other. Each gift has its own distinct way of helping you during your life, and each gift is given by the Holy Ghost. As we just read, "the manifestation of the Spirit is given to every man to profit withal."

The word of wisdom can be given to you for your own private life to help you. Or, other times the word of wisdom will operate through a person to an individual or to a group of people in public assembly. Most Christians don't have it operating in their lives unless they are called into the public ministry, but all Christians could have the word of wisdom operating in their lives for themselves or others. The same gift can operate for you, your friends, or whole groups. It works the same way.

You see, Christians are supposed to be as close together as the parts of the human body are joined together. When we are born again, we become members of the body of Christ. We are brothers and sisters in Christ, and we are supposed to be absolutely in love with each other. God has set the members in the body of Christ exactly where He wants them.

> And if they were all one member, where were the body? But now are they many members, yet but one body. And the eye cannot say unto the hand, I have no need of thee: nor again the head to the feet, I have no need of you.

1 Corinthians 12:19–21

You can't look over to the person next to you and say, "I have no need of you. I've been making it all these years without you. I don't even know you, and I don't need you." You do need them! You need their love. Ten years from now, the person may move next door to you. Then sometime when you're in trouble, the Holy Ghost may give him

52

or her a word of wisdom for you to tell you something that's going to happen to you in the future. The person can walk over to your house, knock on your door, and say, "Oh! I've got to talk to you! The Lord told me something that will happen to you. He showed me in a vision."

That is how God gets His knowledge over to the human race. He is the supernatural God, the spiritual God; we are natural people. He gives His word of wisdom to us through the power of the Holy Ghost within us. And you need the spiritual gift of the word of wisdom working in your life.

Wisdom in Old Testament Men

Back in Old Testament times, most of the old prophets had the word of wisdom operating in their lives to show them what would happen in the future. In fact, the prophet Elisha told the children of Israel all about their enemies. He told them what their enemies were going to do and what they could do about it. (2 Kgs 6:8–12.) God gave a word of wisdom to Noah when He manifested Himself to Noah in Genesis 6. He told Noah that it was going to rain, and then explained in detail how to build an ark.

It didn't rain for over a hundred years, but God told Noah that something was going to happen in the future. Notice here below, beginning with verse 11:

> The earth also was corrupt before God, and the earth was filled with violence. And God looked upon the earth, and, behold, it was corrupt; for all flesh had corrupted his way upon the earth. And God said unto Noah, The end of all flesh is come before me; for the earth is filled with violence through them; and, behold, I will destroy them with the earth.
>
> Genesis 6:11–13

Besides God telling Noah how to build the ark, He told him what to put on it. Noah received that word of wisdom from God. Eight people were saved to replenish the earth as well as every species of animal— "all in whose nostrils was the breath of life" (Gen. 7:22).

Paul and a Word of God's Wisdom

A prime example in the New Testament of someone who availed himself of the gift of the word of wisdom was Paul. Paul received a word of God's wisdom when it looked as though there was no hope. More than forty men had said, "I won't eat or drink until Paul dies!" That's pretty strong! It's bad enough to have two or three men after you to kill you. But when all the leaders say that you will die, and forty men say they won't eat or drink until you're dead, that's serious.

From the natural, how in the world could Paul know what was God's will? Paul was a human being, just like you and me. He didn't know everything in the natural. But Paul had the Holy Ghost living within him. The only thing that Paul knew more than you is what the Holy Ghost gave him through the word of wisdom. Paul also wrote more than half of the New Testament because the Holy Ghost came upon him. The Holy Ghost wrote the New Testament through Paul and others. He gave to them great words of wisdom.

We read in Acts 23:11: "And the night following the Lord stood by him, and said, Be of good cheer, Paul: for as thou hast testified of me in Jerusalem, so must thou bear witness also at Rome." That was all Paul needed!

In other words, Paul said, "I'm not going to die. It doesn't make any difference how many people are fasting for my death or how many leaders say they're going to kill me. I don't care how many jails I'm in, how much blood runs off me, or how badly they beat me! I will preach in Rome because God said that I am to be of good cheer. As I have testified of Him in Jerusalem, so must I bear witness in Rome!"

If you read the life of Paul, you'll find that he always wanted to go to Rome and preach. So he said, "Before I die and leave this earth, I will preach in Rome. God said so, and that's just the way it is!" The gift of the word of wisdom worked through Paul.

Word of Wisdom Through an Angel

God can use you to give yourself a word of wisdom through the Holy Ghost in you. He can use another person to give you the word of wisdom, or He can use angels. Such was the case with Cornelius. God sent an angel to Cornelius' house to tell him what to do, who to talk to, and what would happen if he would obey God. Though Cornelius wasn't saved, he was praying, and God heard Cornelius' prayer.

Many people pray, yet they are not saved. They believe that Jesus is real. They have great respect for God. But nobody has ever taken the time to tell them how to get saved. They only have a vague intellectual vision of God and Jesus. They have a great respect for Him, but have never been born again.

Cornelius was that type of person. He had a good heart about him, but he was not born again. You can read about Cornelius' experience in Acts 10. I will paraphrase it.

Cornelius had been praying up to the throne of God, and the Holy Ghost showed Cornelius what to do. An angel appeared to him and said, "Send some men down to Joppa. There is a man down there by the name of Peter, living a certain house. Ask Peter to come up here. He will give you the words whereby you and your household shall be saved."

That was the point of the word of wisdom. God wanted him to know what would happen in the future because Cornelius had a part to play. Many times an individual has a part to play as to whether something comes to pass or not.

You Need God's Word of Wisdom

It is when God gives you the word of His wisdom to use—to let you know what is going on or what is to take place in the future—that you can talk about being successful in your undertakings. Through the word of God's wisdom, you can find out exactly what you need in your daily life and exactly how the situation is.

In 1 Corinthians 2, we find the revelation of God to man:

And I, brethren, when I came to you, came not with excellency of speech or wisdom, declaring unto you the testimony of God. For I determined not to know anything among you, save Jesus Christ, and him crucified.

And I was with you in weakness, and in fear, and in much trembling.

And my speech and my preaching was not with enticing words of man's wisdom, but in demonstration of the Spirit and of power:

That your faith should not stand in the wisdom of men, but in the power of God.

Howbeit we speak wisdom among them that are perfect: yet not the wisdom of this world, nor of the princes of this world, that come to nought: But we speak the wisdom of God in a mystery, even the hidden wisdom, which God ordained before the world unto our glory.

1 Corinthians 2:1–7

Let me emphasize verse 7: "But we speak the wisdom of God in a mystery, even the hidden wisdom, which God ordained before the world unto our glory." Please study that verse! You can get a glimpse of God's love for you in there. God wants to give you His mind.

Which none of the princes of this world knew: for had they known it, they would not have crucified the Lord of glory. But as it is written, Eye hath not seen, nor ear heard, neither have entered into the heart of man, the things which God hath prepared for them that love him. But God hath revealed them unto us by his Spirit: for the Spirit searcheth all things, yea, the deep things of God. For what man knoweth the things of a man, save the spirit of man which is in him? even so the things of God knoweth no man, but the Spirit of God.

1 Corinthians 2:8–11

You can't get God's ideas on things unless the Holy Ghost gives them to you. The Holy Ghost knows the mind of God—you don't. So if you want to know the real truth about something, you have to get it from the Spirit of God who lives inside of you.

Have you ever heard anybody say, "Well, I thought it was the Lord's will. But it must not have been. This is a mess! I'm not sure it's the Lord's will for me to get married."

Well, if things are a mess, it was not the Lord's will! It was your will. You decided that. The Holy Ghost did not tell you to do it. In fact, that's the problem with most American homes today. God didn't put most husbands and wives together. They put themselves together.

Now we have received, not the spirit of the world, but the spirit which is of God; that we might know the things that are freely given to us of God.

1 Corinthians 2:12

We need to know that the things freely given to us come from the Lord. We do this by allowing our spirit man to listen to the Spirit of God as He gives us the word of wisdom to know what is to come in our lives.

Which things also we speak, not in words which man's wisdom teacheth, but which the Holy Ghost teacheth; comparing spiritual things with spiritual.

1 Corinthians 2:13

That's where people get mixed up. We should not listen to what man's wisdom tells us; we should listen to what the Holy Ghost who lives down in our belly teaches.

But the natural man receiveth not the things of the Spirit of God: for they are foolishness unto him: neither can he know them, because they are spiritually discerned.

1 Corinthians 2:14

If you would ask a person if the Holy Ghost is in his belly, he would think that was foolishness. The natural man cannot receive the things of the Spirit of God. He cannot discern them because they are not naturally discerned.

You can't have the word of wisdom working for you unless you are born again. You need to be born again and baptized with the Holy Ghost. People who live in sin obey the devil. They do not operate the gifts of the Spirit.

But he that is spiritual judgeth all things, yet he himself is judged of no man. For who hath known the mind of the Lord, that he may instruct him? But we have the mind of Christ.

1 Corinthians 2:15–16

If you have the mind of the Lord, you won't make mistakes. I can look back on my past, and there were a lot of situations where I did not have the mind of Christ. I just did things on my own, just like you. You know what I mean. You've done things from the natural standpoint just because you wanted to do it.

We just read that the natural man doesn't understand the things of God. You cannot understand God's will for you in life as long as you're in the natural. Unless you pray and read the Bible, you cannot know the will of God. You may belong to a church, but if you never read the Bible and never pray, you might not recognize God's will. What if somebody knocked on your door and said, "God told me to tell you such and such"? You would not accept it. Why? You would think it was foolishness.

You've got to get in the Word of God and pray so you'll know God's will when you hear it. Then if somebody comes to give you a word of wisdom about what is to come to pass in your life, you can accept it. You will understand that the Holy Ghost is telling you something through that person. You will understand that the Holy Ghost is telling you what will happen to you in the future.

This gift is very important in your life. A word of God's wisdom imparted to you will save you from making a bunch of dumb mistakes and falling into valleys and ditches. It's very important for you to allow this gift to operate through you. Claim it.

A lot of Christians don't understand this and say, "Well, Brother Norvel, how do I get these gifts?" You claim them, just as you do when you claim healing. Say, "Thank You, Jesus. First Corinthians 12 is mine. Thank You, Lord, for the word of wisdom. It is mine. Thank You, Lord, for the gifts of healing. They are mine." God wants to give you a word of wisdom. Today. Now.

Wisdom from God

In the first chapter, I told you about my trip to Howard University in 1971 when I stayed in the house with the priests. Along with a vision of revival the Lord had manifested in me, several gifts of the Spirit were operating, including the word of wisdom.

When the priests left, I knelt down beside my bed to pray. All of a sudden, while I was praying, the Spirit of the Lord showed me a word of God's wisdom. He showed me what He wanted me to do in the future. He wanted me to buy a school bus for a certain pastor, who was over 700 miles away. He plainly showed me that it would come to pass in the future, and that's when God wanted it to be done. "Okay, Lord," I said. "I'll buy the bus, and I went on about my business."

Stand Steadfast

The gift of the word of wisdom may come to you quickly. It may be a few days. It may be a few weeks. It may take months or possibly a few years. But you can know this, when the word of wisdom is imparted to you by the Holy Spirit, He is showing you something that will take place in the future. God wants you to have the wisdom to handle it. Many Christians make the mistake of trying to rush God into doing things, but God has His own timing.

It was about six or seven months after my stay in the Catholic priest's house, when Dr. Lester Sumrall asked me to schedule a meeting for him in South Bend, Indiana. A few months later, I went to South Bend.

Dr. Sumrall took me upstairs in his own house to a room and told me that's where I was going to stay. He told me to make myself at home and the people were going to enjoy my being there. He asked me to let him know if I needed anything. After Dr. Sumrall left me alone in the room, I felt a chill. I knew I needed to pray.

Let me explain that when I stay in someone's home, I always kneel down and ask God to bless that home and all the people in it. I also ask the Lord if He wants to reveal anything to me for them that will encourage and bless them. I tell Him that I will do it. I always want it to be from the Lord. I don't want to get mixed up in family problems. I always pray, "If anybody is going to get messed up in the future, just feel free to use me, Lord. I am available."

There have been many times when God would show me something, and I've walked up to one of the mates and told them what God said. They would begin to cry. I have said, "Now listen, you're not being fair to your husband. The Spirit of God wants me to talk to you." I haven't had a single person yet who hasn't accepted what the Lord gave me through a word of wisdom for them.

As I knelt down and prayed, "God, bless Brother Sumrall. Bless his home and bless the people here, Jesus. Lord, just make me a blessing while I'm here." As I was praying, a word of the Lord came to me saying, "I want you to buy that pastor a school bus."

I said, "Yes, I know You do. You told me that eight or 10 months ago in Washington, D.C., in that Catholic priest's home. I remember what You told me. Jesus, I don't know which school bus You want me to buy. I can't be more honest with You. I'm willing to buy a school bus, but I'm not going to buy a school bus until You tell me which school bus You want me to buy. When You show me the school bus You want me to buy, then I will buy it. If I go ahead and buy a used school bus, You might want me to buy a new one. If I buy a new one, you might want me to buy a used one. You show me the kind of school bus You want me to buy, and I will buy it. Thank You, Lord."

You need to learn this about God: He respects honesty.

I owned the Yellow Cab Company in the city where I lived. I used to get my knees and pray, "Oh, Lord, help me to sell this flaky company. I don't want the Yellow Cab Company. Do You hear me? Please send me a buyer."

He did not send a buyer. I called all the drivers in (there were about eight or ten drivers) when I first bought the company, and said, "Now listen, men. I don't fool around with girls, prostitutes, and whiskey. I know that is how a lot of you guys make your living. I don't make money that way. I don't make my money crooked. The first driver that I find fooling around with girls or whiskey, I am going to fire you. I am not going to tell you twice. I am telling you right now, and that is it. So if that is what you are doing on the side, I am warning you right now, you had better stop it. Don't think that because you got away with it in the past that you can trick me. You may trick me for a while, but I will catch you. The Holy Ghost will show me."

I caught one of them, and I fired him. I liked him the best. I kept the company for eight years and had twenty-four-hour service, seven days a week. I wanted to stop Sunday service, but many elderly people needed cabs to get to church. I decided that if I stopped this flaky company from Sunday service, those people couldn't get to church.

Finally, I decided to close down Sunday afternoons after church. That was hard to do. Cab companies are important to a city. The mayor and the city council wanted it to operate 24 hours a day, seven days a week for emergencies and the like. You may go for ten years and never need a cab, then suddenly at three o'clock in the morning, you need one.

It's always a good thing to have a taxicab company in a city. There was another cab company in town, and we went into partnership together. The other owner was an ex-sheriff of the town. One day, as time went on, we discussed dissolving partnership. I said we could do it on a give-and-take basis. He drew up a contract that said he would pay me so much, and I couldn't start another cab company in Cleveland, Tennessee, for 10 years. I signed the contract. He paid me the amount we had agreed on, and I went down to the bank to deposit the money.

Now it was God's time. As I stepped up to the teller's window, I saw the pastor God had told me to buy a school bus for.

"Hi Pastor!" I said.

He stepped over to me and said, "Where in the world have you been, Brother Norvel? Where has the good Lord taken you since the last time I saw you?"

"All over," I said.

"I don't doubt that!" he said.

"Well, uh..."

He interrupted me. "You know, I was driving down the highway and was going to see the banker tomorrow when, all of a sudden, the

Spirit of the Lord came upon me and told me to go to the bank this afternoon. So I got into my car and came up here."

"What did you come up here for?" I asked.

He said, "Cleveland State College is over here. They have a school bus that they want to sell. They are taking bids on it. The highest bidder will get the bus. I just put in a bid, and when they opened up the box where the bids were placed, my envelope was the only one in there."

By this time, the Holy Ghost was just causing my insides to jump up and down, saying, "This is the bus! This is the bus!"

I remembered my prayer in Lester Sumrall's bedroom, when I said, "Now, Jesus, I'm not going to buy a bus until You show me the one You want me to buy, and I will buy it."

I heard the Lord telling me, "That is what you said."

I said, "Yes, Lord. You are right."

I turned to the pastor and said, "Well, Pastor! Glory to God. I am glad to get this off my mind!"

"Get what off your mind?" he asked.

I said, "The bus, the bus! You wouldn't understand, Pastor. But you don't have to see any banker. Just trust me."

Of course, he knew me really well. We had been together many times before. He said, "I won't do anything until you tell me what you want me to do."

I said, "Come get into my car, and we will go to my office." We arrived at my office, and I told my secretary to write the pastor out a check for the amount of the bus.

God had given me a word of wisdom many months before. Something was to be done in the future, and the time had come for it to come to pass.

Has the Spirit of God been dealing with you and you didn't even recognize it? I can tell you right now what it is. It's a word of wisdom.

If God is showing you something that will come to pass in the future, it's a word of wisdom for you. You're involved in it, and you might as well get ready. If God has shown you something, but you didn't understand until now, then now is the time to yield yourself to God. Tell Him, "I get it now, and I'll do it!"

⏻ Prayer

Jesus, I believe in the gifts of the Spirit. I believe in the word of wisdom. I believe the word of wisdom is a word of God's wisdom coming to me to let me know something God wants to come to pass.

I ask You, Jesus, to help me. I remember that thing that the Lord has been dealing with me about. I remember, Jesus, when You spoke it to me. I give myself to You—totally. I'm available to carry it out anytime You want to bring it to pass.

Thank You, Lord, for giving me a word of wisdom so I won't be deceived. I will carry out the work the Spirit of God wants me to carry out.

I love You, Jesus. I praise You, Jesus. I love 1 Corinthians 12. I thank You for the gifts of the Spirit given to me as the Spirit wills. Thank You, Lord.

Chapter 8

The Word
of Knowledge

What is the gift of the word of knowledge? It is a part of God's knowledge—a supernatural manifestation from heaven—given to a believer. It supernaturally lets us in on information we could not otherwise know; it shows or reveals to us the way things are right now in the present and deals with facts.

The word of wisdom points to the future, but the word of knowledge is about the present. Every one of the nine gifts of the Spirit has its own place. Not one of the other eight gifts can replace the word of knowledge.

If you listen to God and be open and believe that the gift of the word of knowledge is for you, God will let you know the condition of things right now. The word of knowledge doesn't change things for you. You have to learn how to change them. If you don't like the way things are, you can change them totally—that is, if you know how. Most believers, I'm sorry to say, don't know how.

Although I'm not teaching on changing situations here, I will pass on this information. If the condition you're facing is something bad, break the power of the devil. Dedicate yourself to God, claim victory in English, then start praying in tongues until the note of victory comes.

In other words, when God's power shows you the condition of something, the word of knowledge is being manifested to you. If you know how to change the condition, then you can teach somebody else how to change it.

How do you change something that's being destroyed into bright and glorious victory? First of all, if damage is coming as a result of that thing, break the power of the devil over it. "The Lord will break it for me, won't He?" you may ask.

No, He won't break it. You break it. You use Jesus' name yourself. You're a member of God's church. God gave His Son's name to the church to use to take authority over the devil. You break the power of the devil yourself and then claim victory. You must speak victory from your mouth—victory, victory, victory! Then you pray in tongues.

"You mean I should pray in tongues until I see the victory?"

Not necessarily. It could happen that way. But pray in tongues until you see victory or until you get a note of victory.

"How long will it take?"

It might take three or four hours. It might take five or six hours. It took me eight hours one time. Whatever it takes, it's worth it!

I Stayed with It

The gift of the word of knowledge came to me supernaturally in a shopping center in Cleveland, Tennessee. The Holy Spirit said, "Go to Chattanooga, to a certain place."

So, I took off down the highway. When I got to the place, there was a demon-possessed boy who had lost his mind. He had been out streaking or running around with no clothes on, and his mind had snapped. He didn't even know his own name. His daddy was on the way from New Jersey to see him.

A word of God's knowledge came and told me to go there—that's all. God didn't tell me or show me what was there. He could have if He had wanted to, but He didn't want to.

You might ask, "Why doesn't He want to?"

Because He's a faith God. He expects you to move by faith and get victory by faith. When He gives you a few words, you move by faith, and then He will give you more. Sometimes that's easier said than done—especially if He tells you to go across the country.

If Jesus would say, "Go across the country," most people would ask, "What for?" I can tell you now that most of the time, He won't tell them. It's none of their business.

That's the reason perhaps you didn't take some of those trips you were supposed to take, because you wanted to know what for. If God wanted you to know what for, He'd have told you. He didn't, so just forget it. You'll know soon enough. I'll guarantee you that. You'll know when you get there.

I will tell you this: If you'll go when God's word of knowledge tells you to go and do what God's word of knowledge tells you to do, you've never yet been blessed like you'll be blessed. Just follow the instructions that come down from heaven to you. Not only will you be blessed, but also other people will be mightily blessed. You've got to listen to what the Holy Ghost is saying to you. He knows exactly what's going on all the time, everywhere.

I prayed for the boy that was demon possessed for eight hours. I just broke the power of the devil. I said, "Look, thief, (you have to call the devil a thief if you believe he is one), you stole that boy's mind away from him, but you can't have it. Jesus has sent me here to get it back. I came here to stand in the gap for him, to get his mind back. I'm telling you, Satan, I came to take it away from you."

After eight hours, the foam began to run out of the boy's mouth, and his mind snapped back into him. I was determined. God had sent me there under the power of the manifestation of the Holy Spirit that lives inside of me under the gift of the word of knowledge.

God imparted His knowledge to me to do something for Him right then—to go somewhere for Him right then! That's a weapon. That's what the word of knowledge is for. It's a weapon of your warfare against the power of the devil.

You Need the Gifts of the Spirit

Let's read 1 Corinthians 12:7 again: "But the manifestation of the Spirit is given to every man to profit withal." Don't read that verse and think, *I'm not worthy. God wouldn't give me the word of His knowledge. I'm just a little old nothing.*

Don't let the devil beat you down into the ground like that. You have just as much right to the word of God's knowledge as anybody. Do you understand that? You have the Holy Ghost in you, and you have a right. God said that the manifestation of the Spirit is given to every man—and every woman—to profit withal.

You can miss God and miss Him big if you don't listen to the word of God's knowledge. Don't think, *Oh, I'm a Christian. I love God, and Jesus sometimes heals people through me. I have a good relationship with the Lord. I don't necessarily need a word of God's knowledge. I can read the Bible and find out what God wants me to do.* God says to you in verse 21, "And the eye cannot say unto the hand, I have no need of thee: nor again the head to the feet, I have no need of you."

God made you. You're a human being. You belong to God, and you need every one of the nine gifts of the Spirit. In fact, whether you know it or not, you're desperate for them.

You may not feel that you're desperate for them right now, but you will be. There will come a time and place that you will need every one of the nine gifts of the Spirit. They all hold a unique place of their own from God in manifestation to you to bring you success. One cannot replace another one even though some of them operate closely together.

Obey Quickly

One day, a word of God's knowledge came to a pastor's wife in Georgia. She worked for the governor of Georgia, and a word of knowledge came to her at work saying, "Call Norvel Hayes. I want him to come to your church and conduct a meeting for a week or more."

She said, "Yeah, I've heard some of our members talk about him. They've heard him speak somewhere." She got home and told her husband.

He said, "I've never met Norvel Hayes. I don't know him."

"Some of our members do," she said. "Let's find out where he lives."

So they found out and called my office. I wasn't in, of course. I'm hardly ever there. So they talked to my secretary. They explained to her that a word of God's knowledge had come to them telling them that their church needed Norvel Hayes, right now.

When I came in, my secretary told me about it. When they got in contact with me, the Spirit of God said to me, "Go quickly!"

"Yes, Sir," I said.

I didn't know the pastor, and I didn't know the church. But the Lord said, "Go!" so I went to the North Georgia mountains to their tiny church on a gravel road. Talk about back in the boondocks, I had a hard time finding the place. I don't mean it was off on some gravel road—it was *way out* on some gravel road.

When I went in, all the mountain people were singing songs already. The Lord said to me, "Pray." About that time, the pastor came down and said, "Are you Norvel Hayes?"

"Yes, I am," I said. "Do you have some place where I can pray?"

He showed me to a room right off the main room, and I went in there, knelt down, and started to pray. The Spirit of God fell on me supernaturally. I was on my knees crying and praying, and the word of knowledge came unto me, saying, "Get up and go out there and walk back and forth across the front of the church. Do it right now!"

I was sobbing and crying, but I got up and just plowed my way through the door. I went outside and began to walk back and forth across the front of the church, crying and wringing my hands with the Spirit of God all over me.

After I walked for a little while, the power of God fell on the congregation, and they began to shout all over the church—everywhere just shouting and praising God.

They wanted me to stay over for a second week. I told them that I'd let them know on Friday night (that would have been the last service). On Friday morning as I was praying, a word of knowledge came unto me and said, "Stay here for another week." I told the pastor, "God said stay." So I stayed.

One night as I was at the altar just praying for the people, a word of knowledge came unto me saying, "Go back to the city tomorrow and close the deal on that property."

I said, "Property? Property? Oh, yeah. Yes, Lord." I wasn't even thinking about property.

The sum of it was that I got up early the next morning and made my way to my lawyer's office. We drew up the papers and closed the deal on some property. I bought 444 acres of property in the mountains at a few hundred thousand dollars profit.

"Where did you get it?"

I got the word of knowledge in a little mountain church on a gravel road in the North Georgia mountains where I was praying for people, getting them filled with the Holy Ghost, and casting out devils. But what if I had not been receptive to the word of knowledge of God and obeyed Him?

You might say, "I wish God would bless me with $200,000." Have you been to the North Georgia mountains yet?

"No, and I'm not going either," somebody might say.

Well, the Holy Ghost can't do much for you then, because you're too ignorant. Any man who doesn't listen to the Spirit of God just has to wind up working things out for himself.

They needed me in those Georgia mountains, and God used me mightily there. The Lord said to put the gospel first and all these things shall be added unto you.

The word of knowledge comes to you to tell you exactly what to do. You have to listen to Him. Do it now! Don't put it off.

Word of Knowledge in the Bible

I think the greatest Old Testament example of the word of knowledge operating through a person is in the life of Elisha. It probably operated through him stronger than anybody else.

The king of the Syrians had declared war on the king of Israel. But God would give the prophet Elisha a word of knowledge to tell the king of Israel where the enemy army would camp at night.

Elisha would say, "Don't go that way! The enemy army is going to camp there, and they will kill all of you." The king of Israel would send somebody over there after Elisha had told them, and there they were!

Finally, it got to the point that God would impart a word of His knowledge to Elisha, telling him what the Syrian king would say in his bedroom.

Read this carefully! The gift of the word of God's knowledge is available for *you!* You'll be surprised at the things the Lord will let you know the condition of right now through a word of knowledge if you will only believe! You have to believe it, though. And you have to yield yourself to it.

"Yield to what?"

Yield to the Holy Ghost. You can't make God give you a word of knowledge. It comes to you as the Spirit wills.

Let's read this account from 2 Kings 6:8:

Then the king of Syria warred against Israel, and took counsel with his servants, saying, In such and such a place shall be my camp.

He'd tell his servants that. How in the world would Elisha know it? He was on the other side with Israel. He knew it because a word of God's knowledge came unto him and told him.

And the man of God sent unto the king of Israel, saying, Beware that thou pass not such a place; for thither the Syrians are come down. And the king of Israel sent to the place which the man of God told him and warned him of, and saved himself there, not once nor twice.

Therefore the heart of the king of Syria was sore troubled for this thing; and he called his servants, and said unto them, Will ye not shew me which of us is for the king of Israel? And one of his servants said, None, my lord, O king: but Elisha, the prophet that is in Israel, telleth the king of Israel the words that thou speakest in thy bedchamber.

2 Kings 6:9–12

Do you see how strongly the word of knowledge operated in Elisha's life?

Let's look now at the life of Peter and see how this gift operated through him in Acts 10.

> There was a certain man in Caesarea called Cornelius, a centurion of the band called the Italian band. A devout man, and one that feared God with all his house, which gave much alms to the people, and prayed to God alway.
>
> He saw in a vision evidently about the ninth hour of the day an angel of God coming to him, and saying unto him, Cornelius.
>
> And when he looked on him, he was afraid, and said, What is it, Lord? And he said unto him, Thy prayers and thine alms are come up for a memorial before God.
>
> Acts 10:1–4

Remember, Cornelius wasn't even saved, but he prayed every day. God sent an angel to Cornelius' house at the time of prayer. In other words, the angel said, "I've been sent from the Most High God unto you because your prayers and your giving heart have been coming before the throne of God. God has found favor with your prayers and with your giving and with the love you have for people in need."

> And now send men to Joppa, and call for one Simon, whose surname is Peter:
>
> He lodgeth with one Simon a tanner, whose house is by the sea side: he shall tell thee what thou oughtest to do.
>
> And when the angel which spake unto Cornelius was departed, he called two of his household servants, and a devout soldier of them that waited on him continually;
>
> And when he had declared all these things unto them, he sent them to Joppa.
>
> Acts 10:5–8

Cornelius obeyed the word of the Lord that came through the angel. But somebody may ask, "Why didn't the angel tell him how to get saved?" God doesn't save people through angels. He saves people through people.

The word of God's knowledge came to Peter because he prayed. The Spirit of God told him to go pray, so he did. While he was praying, he saw a vision. Then he sat there, thinking on the vision.

Now look at how the word of God's knowledge came to Peter:

While Peter thought on the vision, the Spirit said unto him, Behold, three men seek thee. Arise therefore, and get thee down, and go with them, doubting nothing: for I have sent them. Then Peter went down to the men which were sent unto him from Cornelius; and said, Behold, I am he whom ye seek: what is the cause wherefore ye are come?

Acts 10:19–21

Did you see what Peter asked them? "Wherefore are ye come?" In other words, "I am the one you seek. What do you want?" You might ask, "Why didn't God show him?" God didn't want to show him. God wanted Peter to act by faith and go.

So, Peter went with them to the house of Cornelius, and he opened his mouth and began talking about Jesus:

While Peter yet spake these words, the Holy Ghost fell on all them which heard the word. And they of the circumcision which believed were astonished, as many as came with Peter, because that on the Gentiles also was poured out the gift of the Holy Ghost.

For they heard them speak with tongues, and magnify God.

Acts 10:44–46

The Holy Ghost fell on the whole bunch of them. They were all saved, baptized in the Holy Ghost, and spoke in tongues just like on the day of Pentecost.

Peter was obedient to the word of knowledge. But the word of God's knowledge will not make you do something. God only shares a word of His knowledge with you. You don't have to obey it. But I'll guarantee you, if you will obey it, the greatest blessings that you've ever had in your life will result from it. It may come while you're there, or it may come later on. But I guarantee you, it will come if you obey the word of God's knowledge telling you the condition of something right now. God in heaven will pour out His blessings upon you.

What Is It For?

The Holy Ghost will give you a word of God's knowledge as the Spirit wills. It's for all kinds of things.

One day, one of my restaurants was about to get robbed, and the Spirit willed for me to get a word of knowledge about it. At 5:00 in the morning, God woke me up and brought that restaurant before me, and my spirit became grieved. The Lord said, "Beware today of that one restaurant of yours. Danger!"

That day the restaurant was robbed, and the Lord let me see the man who robbed it. Glory be to Jesus! At 5:00 in the morning, He woke me up and brought it before me. That's what the word of knowledge is for—to show you what's happening in the present—right now.

One night a few years ago in Cleveland, Tennessee, I went into one of my restaurants for pizza with my date. When we got through eating the pizza, we walked outside and got into the car. I was going to take her home. We had just walked a little way when all the sudden the word of knowledge came unto me saying, "Beware! Tonight beware! Danger before you."

I jumped when the Holy Ghost did that to me. I said, "Look everywhere. Look outside. Look back. Look front. God said 'Beware! Danger before us!'"

My date said, "Oh, okay!"

I told her, "A word of God's knowledge came unto me, and He said, 'Beware! Danger is happening right now. Beware!'"

"You know, Norvel," she said, "you're something else."

We drove about a mile when a car pulled out from behind some bushes and was right on my bumper. The Lord said, "That's it!"

I said, "That's it. There's a man back there with a gun in the car."

The police in our town had been trying to get me to carry a gun for years, and I wouldn't do it. I said, "I don't want to carry a gun. I'll just trust the Holy Ghost." And the Lord showed me exactly what to do.

The man's car was very close to mine. In fact, his headlights were almost touching my bumper. I turned right to go to my date's house, which was on a dead-end street. The other car pulled off and turned out his lights. That guy knew I was taking her home, and he knew exactly where I was. The Holy Ghost also knew right where he was. The Holy Ghost knew what tree he was parked behind, and that's the reason the Holy Ghost told me, "Beware!"

God's knowledge came to me to save me from a mess. And a word of God's knowledge *will come to let you know exactly what to do when you need help!*

I pulled my car up in my date's driveway. We went in the house, and I called the police. They came straight to the house.

The other man thought I'd just let her out and come right back, but I didn't. God showed me what to do: go into her house quickly and call the police. I did, and they came. They wouldn't even let me go home alone. The police said, "Mr. Hayes, we're going to go home with you. You know we tried to warn you before. We'd like to give you a gun to carry." They went home with me and looked around the house.

A word of God's knowledge can save you. God will let you know the condition of something right now—this very minute. He will show you exactly like it is—not like you think it might be.

'Get Out and Run'

One night in Columbus, Ohio, I had just left a Billy Graham meeting. A word of knowledge came unto me as I was driving down the street. The Spirit of God came upon me, and I had to park the car. The Lord said, "Pray."

He showed me the condition of a Christian girl who lived in my hometown. She was going to go into a dark cloud. I could see her face. That lasted for about 15 minutes. When I went back to my hometown, I wasn't going to tell her that the Holy Ghost had said, "Beware, don't do what you're going to do. You're in trouble now. Get out and run."

I didn't go the first day and tell her. The next morning when I opened my eyes, my body was hurting so badly, I couldn't get out of bed. God wanted me to go and minister to her, to tell her that the word of knowledge came unto me saying, "Beware and run." I finally got my clothes on and made my way down the steps. I had to hold onto the car to get into it. I finally got to this girl's apartment. I pulled my way up the steps and knocked on the door.

"Jeanie," I said, "I was in Columbus, Ohio, riding down West Broad Street and a word of God's knowledge came unto me. He brought you before me and said to tell you, 'Beware. You're being swept into a dark cloud. Beware! Run, run, run!' What are you doing, Jeanie?"

"I'm not doing anything," she said. "What do you mean?"

"Jeanie, who are you dating?"

"I'm dating a boy that I met down at Daytona Beach, Florida, when I was on my vacation."

"Where did you meet him?"

"I met him down on the beach."

"What was he doing?"

"He was drinking beer."

"Jeanie, you're a Christian, and you love God. What are you dating him for? The hand of God is upon you. A word of God's knowledge came unto me to tell you to beware, Jeanie. Run, run, Jeanie. Get out and run! Run now."

"But, Norvel," she said, "How can I run? He's moved up here from Daytona Beach, and he's living here in Cleveland, Tennessee, now. I'm dating him steadily, and we're thinking about getting married. You haven't seen him, Norvel. He's so good looking."

I said, "The word of God's knowledge came unto me to tell you to run, Jeanie. Beware and run."

About the second or third time I told her, everything was fine. I felt just as light as a feather. I felt like I was about 16. I felt so good from the top of my head to the bottom of my feet when I delivered exactly what God wanted me to deliver—a word of His knowledge to tell her exactly what to do.

"I've done my share, Jeanie," I said. "I'll see you, honey. But you better beware. You better run and run fast."

That was a word of God's knowledge trying to rescue one of His children. But the sad part of this story is that she didn't run. She was a little doll herself, and he was a real nice-looking young fellow; they got married.

I was talking to a girl in the jewelry store one day, and I noticed a young fellow working there. I'd never seen him before. The girl asked me if I knew who he was. I said I didn't.

"That's Jeanie's husband," she told me.

"He's a nice-looking young fellow," I said.

"Isn't he though? Do you know what he is?" she asked.

"No, I don't know what he is. I don't know anything about him."

"He's a gigolo from Daytona Beach. He lives off of old, rich women. He goes to bed with them to get their money. He's been a gigolo for several years. Do you see that black-haired girl standing out there looking in the window now? She acts like she's looking at jewelry, but that's his girlfriend."

I said, "Oh, God, no, not to Jeanie. Oh, Jesus, Jeanie is so sweet. Not to Jeanie."

But the sad part of it is, that was the situation for Jeanie. And it was Jeanie's own fault. She didn't listen to a word of God's knowledge telling her the condition of things and telling her to beware and run.

I saw Jeanie live through five years of hell and heartaches. She had one child. Her husband would stay out all night with some other girl, and she would lock him out of the apartment. She went through five years of that. She finally got sick of him. There was no decency about him, so she left with her little four-year-old girl.

I saw that girl live several years of agony, in torment and hell, because she overrode the word of knowledge. She told me, "Norvel, I've thought about you so much. I've wanted to talk to you so many lonely, disturbed, confusing nights. I would say, 'Jesus, if I could just talk to Norvel and let him pray for me or something.'"

But God didn't deal with me to talk to her anymore. God never told me she was lonely. God used me to give her a word of knowledge not to do it, and she overrode that. She suffered a living hell for several years because of it, but there wasn't any need for it. God didn't want her to suffer.

God doesn't want you to suffer a living hell over several years either. And you don't have to if you'll listen to a word of God's knowledge. It comes to you by the Holy Ghost that lives inside you. It could come to you yourself, or it could come to you through another person.

The gift of a word of knowledge is a revelation gift: God reveals and unfolds His will to you. If you're born again, and you have the Spirit of God in you, the Holy Ghost will give it to you.

But you must treat a word of knowledge—or any gift of the Spirit—as a precious thing. If you don't keep it as a precious thing, it will stop operating. You have to show God respect for His manifestations.

Give Him Up

A pastor came to me one day and asked me to come with him to pick up his daughter at the college campus. I went with him at 3:00 in the afternoon. She got out of class, walked to the car, and got in the back seat. I was in the front seat with the pastor.

As we were going down the highway, all the sudden, the Spirit of the Lord came upon me in the car. A word of God's knowledge came unto me, saying, "Cry and make intercession for her, and I will unfold to her." The Holy Ghost began to cry through me, and I slumped over the dashboard. I began to cry and weep and weep. I cried and prayed all the way to the parsonage.

When we arrived at the parsonage, they got out of the car and went into the house. I sat out there in the car and cried and prayed for an hour. All the sudden, the Spirit of the Lord went into the girl's bedroom and hit her like a bolt of lightning. She came out of the house screaming. She ran and jumped into the car where I'd been praying. She grabbed the steering wheel and started screaming, "I don't want to give him up. I don't want to give him up."

"It doesn't make any difference what you want, you had better," I said.

"Okay, Norvel, okay," she said.

All the sudden, she ended the relationship with her boyfriend. She just cut him off and wouldn't date him. She told me that he nearly went nuts. He almost had gotten her into bed the night before that;

she was so close. But the Holy Ghost came by the word of knowledge to tell her what to do, and she obeyed. She wouldn't go out with him for 12 months.

I thought it was all settled. I thought she had listened to God. A year went by, and she wouldn't even go out with him. Then I heard she was dating him again. It wasn't very long until they were married.

When she was a little child, she was called by God to be a missionary. She had never been to a movie in her life, but after they married they went to sex movies. A missionary ministry was shot down the drain, because she wouldn't listen to a word of God's knowledge.

You better listen when God speaks to you, brother and sister. If you don't, you've got a lot of years of hell to live in.

The gifts of the Holy Spirit in 1 Corinthians 12 are God's weapons against the devil. They are God's weapons for the warfare you're in. The devil and all the demons from hell can't pull a bunch of dumb tricks on you if you listen to the Holy Ghost.

When God speaks, listen!

If you want God to show you the condition of things right now—the way they are—yield now to the Holy Spirit. You have to be available for the Holy Spirit to use you as He wills.

⏻ Prayer

Thank You, Jesus, for 1 Corinthians 12. I don't know everything, but You do! Thank You, Jesus, for a word of God's knowledge coming to me. It's a gift of the Spirit given to me freely when I need it as the Spirit wills. Help me, Jesus, to yield myself to the revelation knowledge of God. Thank You, Lord. I receive in Jesus' name.

Chapter 9

The Gift of Faith

The gift of faith is the first of the three power gifts. It is not the same as regular faith. Hebrews 11:1 talks about regular faith and says, "Now faith is the substance of things hoped for, the evidence of things not seen." But let me tell you here about the gift of faith—a special kind of faith.

I know a woman, a good friend of mine, who is a pastor's wife, and yet she was dying of cancer 25 years ago. Jesus walked into her room and healed her. She has been healed ever since even though the devil has been trying to give her cancer for 25 years. She won't receive it. Symptoms of cancer may come back, but she has faith enough in God's Word that she will get flat on the floor and pray herself through doubt and unbelief and the smog and fog from hell.

Every six months or so the devil will come and try to kill her with cancer, but she won't receive it. She prays until everything leaves her. She prays herself into the glory of God. She prays until God's healing power comes down and surges through her, removing all symptoms from her. That is what you call Hebrews-kind of faith—you believe that God means what He says. Right now! Faith is the substance! She believes that her faith is the substance to health. You can learn to do that on your own.

But that is not the gift of faith. That is not one of the three power gifts of the Spirit. That's not special faith. Actually, there are all kinds of faith. Let me point out some other kinds of faith to you.

A farmer has faith. He sows his seed and believes it's going to come up. That is faith. You exercise faith every time you walk across a busy street expecting cars to stop for a red light. You show faith when you put your money in the bank. You have faith in the honesty and integrity of the bank officers. Why don't you have the same kind of faith in God's Word?

Bible Examples of the Gift of Faith

The gift of faith is a gift of power. I want you to understand how the gift of power works and why God will give it to you. God gives a believer a gift of power because there is something He wants to do. It's always to bless somebody or help somebody. Or, God gives a believer a gift of power to stop something evil.

Let me point out a couple of Bible men who had the gift of faith operating through them. These examples are in the Old Testament.

Daniel had the gift of faith operating in his life. He was a man of God (Dan. 6). When they put him in the lions' den, he was thoroughly convinced the lions would not bite him. Of course, in the morning he was still there. The angel had come and shut the lions' mouths. God's power came, and he knew it. He had the faith. He wasn't a nervous wreck when he went in there because He trusted God.

The gift of faith came upon Samson. He had more power than any human being recorded in the Bible, and God gave it to Samson when he needed it (Judges 15:14–15). A whole army was after him, but Samson killed the whole bunch by himself—hundreds of them with the jawbone of a donkey. Brother, that's power! He had more of God's power than anybody I know of, but it was a gift of the Spirit.

When God sees you're available, He will give you the gift of faith. It's a gift of power to get the job done in whatever situation you're in at that particular time. God doesn't give you all His power. At different times He gives you different amounts of power. He only gives you the amount of power you need to get a job done.

Gift of Faith Brings Healing

Let me explain how the gift of faith operates through a believer's life. The first time it ever operated in my life was for the benefit of somebody else. It operated to keep a Spirit-filled Christian woman from dying.

The woman was sick in her stomach, and she had trouble with her breathing. It kept getting worse. Her husband had to take her to Florida all the time. He had to keep her in Florida for six months sometimes and let her sit out in the sun. It didn't help her stomach any, but it helped her breathing a little.

This woman and her husband were both Spirit-filled and loved God. I was scheduled to be the speaker at the Full Gospel Business Men's Fellowship International (FGBMFI) chapter where the husband was an officer. The wife's name was Helen and she played the piano for conventions. God wanted to use her mightily.

I spoke that night and gave an invitation to pray for people. Helen was one of the first ones in line to be prayed for and came for healing. I prayed for her and all the other people in the line. When I got through praying, I was just standing there. The Spirit of God was working with some of the people. Some were praising the Lord, and some were walking back to their seats.

I noticed where Helen was sitting, and I noticed that she looked so sad. Suddenly, I didn't know what was happening to me, but the moment I looked at her, I began to see her healed. Power came on me, and I got mad at her. She should have been walking up and down the church thanking God for her healing, or at least she should have been sitting in her seat saying, "Thank God, I'm healed! Thank You, Jesus, I'm healed! Glory to God, I'm healed!" But she wasn't. She was sitting with her head down. She looked like she was getting ready to die. I never saw such a sad look on anybody's face.

I looked at her, and the power of God came on me. It was like everybody else in the place just disappeared. I knew they were there, but the gift of faith dropped in me. I could not have cared less what anybody thought. I walked over to her and said, "Helen!" She looked up at me.

"What are you going to do?" I asked. "Sit here and let the devil kill you? Why don't you rise up? I prayed for you in Jesus' name one time! That is all you need, Helen. Do you understand that? You are healed! By His stripes you are healed! Why don't you rise up, Helen? Let God heal you! Why don't you rise up?"

I kept saying that for about 30 seconds while she just looked at me. All the sudden she said, "Okay, Norvel! Okay!"

The power came like the wind and left like the wind. The power wasn't on me anymore. God changed me so quickly, and he restored me back to my normal self just as quickly. It was like the bat of an eye.

Then, the same power that was on me, was on her. She was standing there screaming the victory just like I had been screaming at her. She was screaming, "I'm healed!"

I was just standing there. You know what happens if you obey God, don't you? Immediately, in your mind (that's where the devil operates), the devil starts badgering you. He said to me, "You're nuts! You're crazy! You're a fanatic! They'll never invite you to speak here again, you crazy thing! What are you screaming at that woman like that for? That's not nice." The devil is cunning. He will come to you slick and smooth. That was my first time. I thought, *Oh, what did I do?*

The devil said, "They will never invite you back here to speak. You have just closed the doors for your ministry, because this will get out all over the country. You've had it. You won't get any more invitations, you dummy! You crazy thing! You're getting too wild. You're supposed to be nice."

I thought, *Oh, God, what did I do?* I was ashamed to look at the people. But I did look at them. Some of them were looking at me and some at her.

She was still standing there screaming, "I'm healed!" The power had gone from me into her, but I didn't know that until about a week later. There was a convention a week later not very far away. I thought I would go up one day to see who was speaking and enjoy the service. I walked into the auditorium where there were several hundred people, and Helen was playing the piano.

When she saw me come in, she stopped playing the piano and jumped off the stage. She ran down the aisle to me and said, "Brother Norvel, I'm healed! I'm healed completely! Everything has disappeared. I went out that night and ate a T-bone steak, and I digested it. It's the first time I've digested food in six months. I've eaten anything I've wanted to since that night, Brother Norvel. Every symptom has disappeared from me. I breathe real good, and my stomach is completely healed. Look at my face, I'm getting my color back. My cheeks are already turning rosy. I've gained about nine pounds since that night. Norvel, do you remember me? Do you remember that night when you were screaming at me?"

"Yeah, honey," I said. "I remember when I was screaming at you."

She said, "You probably don't know what happened. While you were screaming at me that power started coming from you into me. That power that went into me caused me to be strong enough and bold enough to start confessing my healing boldly. When I started confessing my healing boldly, I got healed. All the afflictions disappeared!"

87

The gift of faith is what did it. I know the gifts of healing followed it when she started confessing her healing. But the gift of faith changed me into another person to make her think differently. The gift of faith caused a woman who had been eating only baby food for six months to start eating normally and not die! God gave me the power to talk to her like that, so she could start believing the Bible and rise up against that thing. You have to rise up against the devil. I don't care what kind of works the devil tries, you have to rise up against him!

Set the Captives Free

The gift of faith can operate through you for a demon-possessed person, especially if the person is crying out for help and wants to be free. Let me tell you about a time the gift of faith operated through me.

A Christian girl in our town was hanging around with the wrong boys and started going to bed with them. She was raised as a Spirit-filled Christian and knew better, but she got in so far she couldn't get out. She'd tell herself every day, "I'm not going to bed with this boy tonight. I'm not going to do it." But she would go out and wind up doing it every night.

She started visiting churches, knocking on church doors, and asking for help. Most pastors were really nice and prayed for her. But you don't pray for a demon-possessed person. You cast the devil out of them!

I was planning to go to a convention, but the Lord let me know that He didn't want me to go to the convention. He wanted me to go to a prayer meeting Wednesday night. There were a few people there, and the pastor preached and gave an invitation. This girl got up out of her seat and went down to the front altar. The Spirit of God said in me, "Go pray with her."

So I did. I got down on my knees beside her and prayed with her. She was crying out for help. She cried, "Help me, Jesus. Some way help me, Lord."

I was praying, "Help her, Lord," but thought to myself, *What's wrong with her?* I was the only one up there praying. I prayed about 15 minutes, I think. Right toward the end, one or two more came up, knelt down around her, and started praying. I felt I didn't want to pray anymore, so I got up off my knees and went back to my seat.

I was sitting there, minding my own business, and the Lord began to roll around in my spirit the 16th chapter of Mark—the Great Commission.

Go ye into all the world, and preach the gospel to every creature. He that believeth and is baptized shall be saved; but he that believeth not shall be damned. And these signs shall follow them that believe; In my name shall they cast out devils.

Mark 16:15–17

What stood out to me was, "In my name shall they cast out devils." I said, "Please, Lord Jesus, in this particular church, I don't think they cast out devils."

"The 16th chapter of Mark casts them out."

"Lord, I don't have enough power to do that," I said. "Don't make me do that. I have friends here. Besides that, Lord, I don't run this church. I don't think they do that in here."

"The 16th chapter of Mark does. In My name they shall cast out devils. Those that believe in Me, in My name, they shall cast out devils," the Lord said.

"Yes, Lord, yes." I was crying by that time. He just kept rolling Mark 16 around in front of me, just like He had a one-track mind. I wanted the Lord to get over in the book of Matthew or Luke, but He didn't go anywhere. He just stayed in the 16th chapter of Mark and the Great Commission.

"Yes, Lord, I know it's in there," I said. All the time I was trying to talk to Him, He wasn't even listening.

After a while, I said, "Lord, I work for You."

"I know you do. I hear you going around the country saying that you love Me. 'Oh, I love Jesus. Jesus has done so much for me. Let me tell you what He's done for me.' Tonight I demand you show me!"

Words are cheap. I already knew what He wanted me to do, but I was trying to get out of it. But He started melting me. He said, "Look at that girl at the altar, crying out for help. Look at her, son. She's crying out for help, and nobody has helped her. She's been to church after church after church, and she's still crying out for help."

Jesus said, "Look at her! I want to help her through you." This got me. I absolutely couldn't take it. He said to me just so plainly, "It doesn't make any difference to Me now, the past is past. It doesn't make any difference to Me how many boys she's been to bed with. I love her, and she's crying out for Me. I love her, and I love all of those like her. If you are going to work for Me, you had better not forget that. I didn't put that evil spirit in her that makes her do the things she does. The devil put it in her. The devil has gotten in her. I want you to go up there and use My name, and cast that thing out of her."

"Jesus, I'm not ashamed of You," I said.

"Show Me. If you're not ashamed of the 16th chapter of Mark, you're not ashamed of Me. If you are ashamed to obey it, you're ashamed of Me. If you're not ashamed of Me, and you love Me, show Me. I love her. I want to help her."

I said, "Jesus, You have the power. I know You have the power. Go ahead and help her, Lord."

"I work through My Word. I work through believers. I'll do what you do. You obey the 16th chapter of the book of Mark, and I'll be with you."

Remember what Jesus told the disciples? He didn't say, "I'll go before you and do all the work." He said, "I'll go with you, confirming the Word with signs following."

"Give me power, Jesus, and I'll do it!" I said. "I'll do anything You tell me to do, if You'll give me power." I meant business.

As soon as I said that, on the inside of my belly, the Holy Ghost began to rise up, like somebody blowing up a balloon. The power began to come into me. I had power in my fingers. I had power in my hands. I had power in my arms. I had power in my chest. Even my eyes were full of power. I couldn't see anything except victory! My mouth was full of power! Everything about me was full of power.

When the power came on me, I got up out of my seat. I walked down front like I was going to battle. As I got down there, a guy was standing close to her, and I told him, "Have her stand up because God is going to set her free!"

"Stand up, young lady! Stand up!" he told her.

I put my hand on the side of her head and said, "You foul spirit that has wrecked this girl's life, in Jesus' name, come out of her!" I said it one time. It was like the wind. It had to be a demon—whoosh! Her body went back through the air and hit the floor. She landed flat on her back. The moment she hit the floor, tears gushed out of her eyes, and she started speaking in tongues just as fast as she could. The gift of faith made the difference. It gave me power to get the job done. The people all shouted and rejoiced and praised God.

Several months later the pastor of that church called me and said the girl was getting married. "She wants you to read the Bible at her wedding," he said.

I went to the wedding that was in her house. As the music started, she came around the corner marching to *Here Comes the Bride*. As I looked at her, the Spirit of the Lord came upon me. Tears were streaming down my cheeks as Jesus so softly and sweetly spoke to me. He said, "Thank you, son, for obeying the 16th chapter of Mark and for casting the devil out of her. Now she comes to be married, and she stands before Me clean and white as snow. She stands before Me as though she had never sinned." Glory be to God!

Can you imagine Jesus thanking me for doing something? You know what it means for Jesus to come to you and thank you? I want to thank Him for what He has done for me. Praise the blessed name of the Lord God forever because of the gift of faith!

Gift of Faith Brings Salvation

Some people called me from Philadelphia and wanted me to come to a business meeting. Between the sessions, they dismissed us to go eat. We walked into a restaurant and didn't have any reservations. When they called out "table for two," the man who was lecturing at the meeting and I just stepped out and sat down at a table together.

I'm a Christian businessman. It's just a normal thing to me to sit down and say, "Well, thank You, Jesus. Praise the Lord. Isn't Jesus good?"

The man looked at me and said, "Mr. Hayes, I want to tell you something. I don't believe in that kind of stuff."

"You don't believe in God?"

"No!"

"Why not?" I asked.

"People say that God is love."

"He is."

"Oh, yeah? My wife is an alcoholic, Mr. Hayes. I have a 12-year-old son and a 14-year-old son. My 14-year-old son is a dope addict. If God is love, He sure didn't stop at our house. Why should I believe in Him?"

"You have to believe God," I said. "You have to show God faith that you believe in Him. God will give you whatever you want." Then I started giving my testimony, telling him what God had done for me. It was like water running off a duck's back. He didn't believe a word of it.

"It may be true, but I doubt it. It probably just turned out that way for you. I don't believe it," he said. He let me know my testimony didn't even phase him.

We finished eating and walked up the sidewalk to the meeting room. I was minding my own business, talking to him. Some of the other men were walking in front of us, and some were behind us. All the sudden, power fell on me and changed me into another man!

God gave me words to say to him. I wheeled around, got him by the arm, and pulled him around. I stuck my finger in his face and said, "Listen, Mister, God's real regardless of what you believe! Jesus told me to tell you that He doesn't want your two sons to die and go to hell. If you don't introduce them to Him, when you die and go to hell, He will hold you responsible for them!" Then I just turned around and walked off. He stood there looking like I had hit him with a stick.

I went in and sat over against the wall. He came and sat at the desk, because he was the lecturer. I looked over at him, and the gift of faith came upon me—power came upon me, again. This time it was a different type of manifestation. The first time on the sidewalk was authority. This time the Spirit of God began to move on my innermost being, and I began to cry and weep. Compassion boiled up out of me. The power was all over me. The Lord said to me, "Walk over there and pray for him right now."

Some of the other men had come in and were sitting around. I just walked across the floor crying. I walked up to his desk and said, "As I was sitting against the wall, the Spirit of the Lord came upon me. Jesus loves you, and He wants me to pray for you. Bow your head and close your eyes, and I'm going to pray for you right now." I was crying. He looked up at me, and my hands were up.

He said, "Oh, okay."

I reached up and touched him on the top of the head, and I said, "Jesus, touch this man. Jesus, give this man another life. Touch him!" His head fell down onto the desk like he'd been hit with a hammer. He started crying as soon as his head hit the desk. He was crying and weeping.

I said, "Tell Jesus you are sorry for your sin. Ask Jesus to come into your heart, Mister, right now. The Spirit of the Lord is all over you. Ask Him to come into your heart!"

He said, "Jesus, come into my heart." He just cried and wept and sobbed on the top of the desk. There he was getting born again when five minutes before he didn't believe in God.

You might say, "Norvel, that was a good job. You really did the right thing, didn't you?" Are you kidding? I told him everything I knew, and it didn't phase him. My knowledge of God couldn't even get to him. It was a gift of power that God gave that made the difference.

A year later I was sitting on the stage at a FGBMFI convention in Phoenix, Arizona. I saw a guy walking up the aisle grinning from ear to ear. He jumped up on the stage where I was sitting and walked over to me. He said, "Brother Norvel, it's wonderful. God is wonderful. Jesus is wonderful."

"Yeah, I know He is. I know He's wonderful."

"Don't you remember me—Philadelphia, Pennsylvania?" he asked.

"Oh, dear Lord! Yeah, I remember you."

"Do you know what happened to me?"

"No," I said.

"I went home to my alcoholic wife," he said. "I told her, 'I met this strange man. He put his hands on my head and something came in me and knocked me on the desk. I began to cry and weep.' I told her that I got saved. Then she got saved. I told my dope-addict son, and he got saved. My son got filled with the Holy Ghost. I got filled with the Holy Ghost. My wife is here. My son is going to Bible school. All my relatives are saved. I moved from Philadelphia to California. And I'm the president of a FGBMFI chapter in California now."

I said, "You mean all in one year?"

"It doesn't take me long to do something," he said.

God wanted to save him. You might say, "Why did God save him?" Because I was available for the gift to operate through. The gift of faith came upon me. The power was on me. The power went from me into him when I touched him on the top of his head. The gift of faith can change people. The Spirit of God can change people through the gift of faith, but God has to have believers to operate through.

It's a supernatural gift! It's available for the Church.

It's available for *you!*

But the gift of faith will never operate through you unless you make yourself available, so make yourself available to the Lord!

Prayer

Jesus, I'm available for the gift of faith. I'm available to be changed into another person to help somebody, to bring healing to somebody, to bring salvation to somebody, to stop the evil works of the devil, and to bring the glory of God into manifestation on the earth. I'm available for God's power to come upon me and change me. I'm available.

I love You, Jesus. I love the gospel. Mold me into the person You want me to be. I believe in 1 Corinthians 12. I believe the gift of faith is a gift of power that God gives to believers to get the job done. Thank You, Jesus, I'm free from unbelief.

Chapter 10

The Gifts of Healings

One of the power gifts is called the gifts of healings. I know the King James Version of the Bible lists this as *"gifts of healing,"* but in the Greek both words are plural—*gifts of healings*. Why is it plural? Because there are many kinds of sickness, and many things cause sickness. Some sicknesses are caused by accidents, some by personal neglect, some by organic ailments, some by a spirit of infirmity, some by satanic oppression, and some by demonic possession.

Yet, a gift of healing is God's power flowing down through your body to drive out afflictions in Jesus' name no matter where or how the sickness comes. It's a gift of healing that God drops in people, but it's not manifested in the same way all the time.

Sometimes God's healing power drops on you, and your body just unfolds before Him. You just drop on the floor. Sometimes it drips on you, and it comes so easy and precious and sweet and warm. Sometimes God's healing power will drop on you, but you won't even feel anything. You have to check yourself and find out that you're healed.

But when a gift of healing comes, it comes so quickly. It's given as the Spirit wills. You never know when it's going to happen. A gift of healing works differently. It's still God's healing power—don't get me wrong. It's the same kind of healing power that comes when a person lays his hands on somebody, but it usually comes in a stronger way.

There are all kinds of ways for you to be healed. The laying on of hands is just one way to be healed. Some people receive God's healing power and the gifts of healings, and nobody touches them. They don't necessarily try to quote anything; it just comes to them automatically. That's involved in the gifts of healings that's given out as the Spirit wills (1 Corinthians 12). When it comes, it just comes.

What is it? It's an amount of power that God chooses to give as He manifests Himself. You might ask, "Why doesn't God give it to everybody who's sick?" I don't know. The late Kathryn Kuhlman, a well-known healing evangelist, said one time, "When I get to heaven, I'm going to ask Jesus, 'Why do two wheelchair cases get up and walk off, and 10 don't?'"

I don't think anybody in the world completely understands it. I discussed it with Brother Hagin, and he doesn't. Neither do I. The only thing I can tell you is that there's a gift called the gifts of healings in 1 Corinthians 12, and it's available for the Church.

But God only gives out His healing power where healing scriptures are taught. God only gives His healing power out where somebody is bold enough and honest enough to stand up for God and say, "Jesus is your Healer, and He wants to heal you right now."

Healing for All

You've got to tell people that Jesus paid for their healing on the cross. You've got to tell people that healing is available to them and belongs to them. People can only believe what they've been taught.

I prayed three days one time, trying to get God to tell me why my mother died with cancer at the age of 37. On the third day of praying, the Word of the Lord came unto me saying, "I didn't kill your mother with cancer, son. I didn't have anything to do with it. I couldn't give your mother cancer anyway, because I live in heaven; there are no cancers in heaven."

"Jesus," I said, "She was a good Christian. She loved You. She was Your child. Why did she die at 37 years of age?"

I don't want to make you mad, but Jesus said, "Where she went to church, nobody ever taught her how to be healed. Nobody ever taught her how to receive My divine healing that flows down from heaven to the believer. She's in heaven now, but nobody taught her how to be healed."

You'd better make sure that the church you go to is one that Jesus built. Jesus said, "The church that I build, the gates of hell shall not prevail against it" (Matt. 16:18). The work of hell isn't even supposed to work in the church that Jesus builds. It's supposed to be thrown out by the leaders of the church. There's supposed to be enough of God's Word going forth to demolish anything the devil tries to do to a church member.

You may have thought that relative of yours who died young with a disease died because it was time, and the Lord came and got your relative and took him or her home. Is that what you thought? Almost everybody thinks that unless they've studied the Bible. They don't know any better, so they just think it was God's time.

Always remember as long as you live: God does what you do. God's power is available for everybody. If you have a short leg, God's power is available to make it long. If you need something new in your body, God's power is available to give it to you. If you've got a disease in your body that you've had for a long time, there's no reason for it to stay any longer. The power of God is available for you if I can talk you into believing it.

I was raised in a denomination that never taught me about God's healing power. That's the reason I didn't know anything about it. I hadn't been taught that God's healing power is a free gift to everybody.

We had our own slant, our own version of it. We believed Jesus could heal people if He chose to do it. But we believed it might be God's will to heal somebody, and it might not be God's will to heal somebody else. That kind of thinking is not scriptural.

If you're reading this and you're really healthy—not even one small thing wrong with any member of your body—you might say, "I'm healed. I really don't need this." But listen to me. If you'll learn this now and get it into your spirit now, when the devil comes to your body, you can throw him out. So learn right now while you're healthy and strong.

Smith Wigglesworth said in his writings that if you wait until you're flat on your back with a disease before you try to believe in God's healing power and accept your healing by faith, you've waited too long.

If you wait until you're flat on your back, you can't then start learning about faith for healing. You're having to fight that affliction and fight that pain and fight that disease 24 hours a day. The symptoms are so strong in your body, they take your attention. You can't give enough attention to God's Word. You haven't taken the time to memorize those healing scriptures. You haven't taken the time to put them down in your spirit. They are not a part of you.

Remember, the only scripture that ever works for you is the scripture that becomes a part of you, like your right arm. It has to be attached to you. It has to be so embedded in you so it can't come out of you.

You may say, "I don't have God's healing scriptures in me that strong." Then hunt some up in the Bible and quote them about a thousand times. Go around for about a month saying, "Jesus is my Healer." But do it while you're strong, well, sharp, and healthy.

Then when the devil comes, you'll look at him and say, "Jesus is my Healer," because you've got it in your spirit so strong. It just comes out of you. You have something to use against the devil.

But as long as you take the Bible and just nonchalantly try to believe it—doing what you want to do—you'll be robbed of God's healing power. You won't get healed either. You'll have to put up with it and spend all your money on hospitals and doctors.

Jesus Ministered Healing

I want to show you two of the different ways that the Lord healed people when He was here on earth. If you're a good student of the Scriptures, you'll find out that Jesus had all the gifts of healings operating through Him. Jesus had healing power working through Him to heal everybody. He healed all kinds of diseases (Matt. 8:16).

Let's read in Matthew 17:

And when they were come to the multitude, there came to him a certain man, kneeling down to him, and saying,

Lord, have mercy on my son: for he is lunatick, and sore vexed: for ofttimes he falleth into the fire, and oft into the water.

And I brought him to thy disciples, and they could not cure him.

Then Jesus answered and said, O faithless and perverse generation, how long shall I be with you? how long shall I suffer you? bring him hither to me.

And Jesus rebuked the devil; and he departed out of him: and the child was cured from that very hour.

Then came the disciples to Jesus apart, and said, Why could not we cast him out?

And Jesus said unto them, Because of your unbelief: for verily I say unto you, If ye have faith as a grain of mustard seed, ye

shall say unto this mountain, Remove hence to yonder place; and it shall remove; and nothing shall be impossible unto you.

Matthew 17:14–20

Does Jesus say to His Church, to believers, "And nothing shall be impossible unto you?" Does Jesus say that or doesn't He?

Of course, with that case you thought was impossible and all your friends thought was impossible, you got what you believed. That's the very reason you got what you believed—you thought it was impossible. Listen, you don't get victory unless you believe victory and talk victory. Then victory comes.

Howbeit this kind goeth not out but by prayer and fasting.

Matthew 17:21

You might say, "I don't know why I couldn't make this disease leave." Or, "I don't know why I couldn't get this lunatic healed." Or, "I don't know why I couldn't get this person healed that the devil was attacking."

You have to recognize if a disease has been caused by a devil, by natural things, or by your ignorance or neglect (like getting wet and sitting in front of the air conditioner).

If it's the dumb devil that has tried to possess you, take you over, or oppress you, you need to deal with that spirit and cast it out. Demons cause sicknesses, too. They will come to kill you.

Always remember this: If it's a deadly disease, always take authority over the spirit of death. Death is the enemy of God. Take authority over it, break the power of the devil, and claim God's healing power. Always do that when you're dealing with a devil of oppression or possession.

When you're dealing with a spirit that's a killer, you need to fast and pray some, so you'll have power over that thing and make it obey you. Some spirits just will not obey you unless you fast and pray.

If you think you can go along and just break the power of the devil and get all kinds of diseases healed and all kinds of goofed up people restored back to normal, I've got news for you. You can't do it with some of them unless you fast and pray. Jesus said right there, "Howbeit this kind goeth not out but by prayer and fasting." It all depends on what kind you're dealing with.

If you're dealing with a regular disease, God's healing power can drive it out of you— literally, drive it out of you.

While I've been speaking on God's healing power, the gifts of healings have begun to manifest, and devils have fits. Devils leave and people get completely healed. Devils leave and crooked legs straighten out. When God's power starts dropping on the congregation, all kinds of things happen.

But you can see that the boy Jesus healed was put in that shape by the devil. The devil did it.

Let's look at another Bible case in Luke 13:

And he was teaching in one of the synagogues on the sabbath. And, behold, there was a woman which had a spirit of infirmity eighteen years, and was bowed together, and could in no wise lift up herself.

Luke 13:10–11

She had a spirit of infirmity. Where does that come from? It comes from the devil who can cause diseases and afflictions upon you.

And when Jesus saw her, he called her to him, and said unto her, Woman, thou art loosed from thine infirmity. And [notice this now: a doctrine of the Church] he laid his hands on her: and immediately she was made straight, and glorified God.

Luke 13:12–13

They started making fun of Him for healing her, but notice what Jesus said:

> And ought not this woman, being a daughter of Abraham, whom Satan hath bound, lo, these eighteen years, be loosed from this bond on the sabbath day?

> Luke 13:16

Both of the conditions mentioned in this chapter were caused by the devil. The woman got healed by the laying on of Jesus' hands. The boy who was lunatic got his healing because Jesus cast the devil out of him.

God wants you healed. He always wills to heal you, and He has provided many different ways for you to get your healing. I just wanted to show you two of the ways the Lord heals people.

Specialists

I've never known anybody in the ministry except Jesus who could leave 5,000 sick people—crippled, blind, demon possessed, and lunatic—with every one of them healed.

Almost every person God gives a healing anointing to minister has at least one—and sometimes two or three—specialties. I mean, the minister just has absolutely wonderful results with a few particular ailments especially.

I know a fellow in my hometown who used to be a midget. "What do you mean *used to be* a midget? You mean he's not a midget now?" No, he's not. He's now 6 feet, 1 inch tall and weighs about 190 pounds.

I've known his family all my life. I went to school with his sisters. Jimmy was a little boy who just stopped growing when he got to be 12 years of age. The doctors couldn't figure it out—nobody could. He weighed 92 pounds when he was 12 years old. When he went to be examined for the army (of course they didn't take him), he still weighed 92 pounds. I think he was 4 feet 9 inches tall then.

God called him to work with little children. He said, "God, I don't want to work with those little kids. I want to be big. Get yourself another man."

One day, when he was 26 years old, he was driving down the road at about 35 or 40 miles per hour. A drunk came driving down the highway doing about 95 miles per hour, and they had a head-on collision. The boy who was the passenger was killed. Jimmy's legs were knocked out of their sockets, and his thigh bones, driven through his hips, were sticking out. He was crushed, but for some unknown reason, he was still breathing.

They took him to the hospital, but they said they couldn't help him. They thought he would be dead in a few minutes anyway. They suggested that perhaps someone in Chattanooga could help him, but he'd probably die before he got there.

They took him to a big hospital in Chattanooga. The doctor there said, "There's no way we can help him. He won't live. There's no use in trying to operate on him. He's too crushed. Just put him in a room over there. He'll be dead by morning."

He had been unconscious, but he opened his eyes and said to Jesus, "Lord, don't make me meet You like this. I know You tried to get me to win souls for You, Jesus, but I never have won any. Jesus, if You'll heal me, I'll knock on doors for You. I'll win souls for You for the rest of my life, Jesus, if You'll heal me." Then he lost consciousness again.

To the doctor's amazement, Jimmy opened his eyes the next morning. He had lost about a gallon of blood. The doctor said, "I can't understand how this boy is still breathing. He even acts like he's alert this morning."

Do you know that Jesus makes blood? Do you believe that God's power can do anything? Do you believe that Jesus would have compassion on a little midget boy laying in the emergency room, crying out for mercy?

A few days later, there he was, still living. Six or seven days later they put 35-pound weights on his feet and started pulling his bones back through his hips. They kept him in the hospital for months.

One day when the doctor and nurse thought Jimmy was asleep, the doctor said, "You know it's a shame what's happened to this little fellow. He seems like a nice little fellow. But even if he lives through this, he'll never be able to walk again. Of course, I personally don't think he's going to live."

The devil took that statement and bombarded his mind with it: *You'll never walk again. You'll be a cripple the rest of your life.* Jimmy became afraid that he'd never walk again.

Finally, they sent him home. Reading the Bible one day, Jimmy saw that God had not given him a spirit of fear, but of power, love, and a sound mind (2 Tim. 1:7). He started reading where Jesus healed people. He started believing that Jesus was his Healer. He took authority over the spirit of fear and made it leave him.

The ambulance came and got him once a week for about nine months and took him to the hospital. Toward the end of the nine months, he found in the Bible that he could take authority over the devil. Two weeks later, after he broke the power of the devil over himself, his legs and body began to grow. He got up and started walking around. Every 30 days he'd look down and his pants were too short. He had to go and buy new trousers every 30 days because he grew so fast. He grew from about 4 feet 9 inches to 6 feet 1 inch in 10 months.

That's really the number one way to be healed! Find scriptures and just stand on them yourself. Just tell God that you believe it and stand on it. I believe God will do anything for you. I believe He loves you that much. All things are possible to him who believes.

The Lord has given Jimmy a ministry. I would say 95 percent of the people who have bad backs that he lays hands on and prays for get their healing. God just gives the people brand new backs. At least nine out of ten get their healings. God does that sometimes. There are certain things that seem to work stronger through some people's ministries. God's healing power works through them to heal many people, but they have specialties to get people healed of particular diseases.

It seems with me, it's bad hearts and crooked limbs where I really see results. Sometimes people walk up to me in conventions with some of their limbs crooked. I just start to pray for them, and they are made normal, right in front of my eyes. Don't ask me why it works that way with some people. I don't know why, but it does. Sometimes God deals with me mightily at different places about people with bad hearts. He wants to give them new hearts, and He does.

He came on me strongly one time in Indiana at a convention. I was just sitting there, and my heart started hurting. I couldn't take it any longer. It felt like my heart was going to stop. I knew what it was. God had already shown me. The emcee was talking about different things. I mean, it wasn't important what he was saying. He could have said it the next day. But I was sitting there with my heart hurting so badly, I couldn't take it any longer. The Lord said, "Right now!"

So I got up and called all the people with bad hearts down to the front. If I'm not mistaken, there were ten of them. They were standing there, and all the sudden, God's healing power just dropped on them. God began to heal their hearts and give them new hearts. All of them fell over on the floor, right in front of the convention. Nobody even touched them. The gifts of healings work different ways at different times, but it's still all God's healing power.

Jesus Confirms the Word

The Bible says that the Lord confirms the Word with signs following (Mark 16:20). But the gifts of healings in 1 Corinthians 12 are given out as the Spirit wills.

Let me explain it this way. God always wills to heal you—always. God will always confirm His healing promises in His Word when you take hold by faith. You can take hold of promises in God's Word anytime, anywhere. But God doesn't always will to manifest Himself through the gifts of healings (drop it on somebody by His sovereign will). That doesn't change the fact that God always wills to heal you.

The gifts of healings, given out as the Spirit wills, manifest a lot of times when I'm teaching the Bible. Now it doesn't happen really often, but over a number of years, it has happened a lot of times.

With my own eyes, I saw a supernatural healing happen when I laid my hands on a person in an Assembly of God church in Mississippi. I was praying for sick people on Sunday night after I had taught on healing. I came to a man who said so simply, "Mr. Hayes, skin cancer is all over my body. I want Jesus to heal me."

I reached out and said, "I curse this cancer in Jesus' name. I want to thank You, Jesus, for giving him new skin." I'm sure I didn't pray for him for over 30 seconds. Then I went on to the next person.

He turned around to sit back down on the front bench and just said, "Thank you." He didn't notice anything. But when he started to sit down, he saw new skin was on him, and he jumped up.

He said, "Everything has disappeared! I've got new skin on me! People, new skin has come upon me!"

People started breaking down, crying. It was the most simple thing you've ever seen in your life. The Lord put new skin on him. When God's healing power falls on the congregation and starts to heal the people, that's the gifts of healings.

One time I was teaching at a university and it happened. I was just teaching the Bible, minding my own business. All the sudden, some woman jumped up and shouted, "It happened right there! It happened right there!"

I looked back, and this real fancy, socialite-type woman was standing back there looking at her chair. I said, "Lady, what happened right there?"

"I've been deaf for 30 years," she said. "When you were teaching the Bible, you pointed here to where we were sitting. You said real strong, 'God will do anything for you if you'll believe Him.' All the sudden, when you said that, my ears went *bloop*. I started hearing everything, and it happened right there."

One time I was teaching at the University of Florida. One night I started praying for the sick, and God's healing power was flowing strongly. A professor was there who came up. God healed him right in front of the congregation.

His daughter was visiting from New York. He said, "My daughter's got a disease. Would you be willing to pray for her?"

"Oh sure," I said.

When she came up, God laid her out the floor and healed her. The professor and his daughter both were healed completely. The girl went back to New York and told a bunch of people in Kingston, New York, "I met this fellow, and God heals people when he prays for them. The Lord healed my daddy, a professor at the University of Florida, and He healed me. Tell some of the pastors. Write him a letter and ask him to come up here to Kingston."

Before long, they wrote me a letter. The Spirit of God dealt with me to go up there, so I went. The ministers in that city had a meeting once a week. They would get together and have breakfast and pray together. The Lutheran minister told me that he agreed to let them use his church. It was one of those beautiful, fancy churches. It had really dark wine-colored carpet. There were two pulpits. One was way up in the air. You had to climb steps around the back to get to it.

I sat there wondering, *Do I have enough nerve to climb those stairs?* Right before they introduced me, I decided I had enough nerve. (I had always wanted to do that anyway.)

I spoke, and the first night 26 people came forward to get saved. I gave just a plain salvation invitation, and they jumped up out of their seats and rushed down front to get saved.

Then, when I gave an invitation for healing, there must have been 40 people who came forward. They were standing at the altar. All the sudden, a boy 22 or 23 years of age, who was supporting himself with two crutches, lifted both arms and his crutches fell. He turned and walked right down the middle of the church. He went past a blind boy, and the boy's eyes popped open. Thank You, Jesus, for the gifts of healings.

The gifts of healings are God's healing power flowing down through your body to drive out afflictions in Jesus' name, and they come as the Spirit wills. Of course, when you teach this gift, the Spirit always wills to manifest Himself in the gifts of healings.

You can accept your healing right now, on your own. You see, you can accept it from God's Word. That's the reason I pointed out several ways for you to be healed.

More Than One Gift

The Bible calls it the *gifts* of healing, not the *gift* of healing. It's plural because God gives many different kind of healings and delivers them to you in many different ways. Sometimes God anoints a ministry gift with a certain type of healing gift. For example, Brother Hagin had great success with getting people healed from tumors. Healing also can be transmitted by the laying on of hands or by anointing with oil.

The thing to remember with the gifts of healing is that it's as the Spirit wills. When 1 Corinthians 12 is preached, taught, and expounded upon boldly in the sanctuary, the gifts will often spontaneously manifest. Someone sitting in the sanctuary might be healed. The gifts of the Spirit operate as God wills, and the Spirit always wills.

Doing miracles is not God's number one way to heal people. God's number one way to heal you is for you to believe Him yourself. You have to believe that the Lord Jesus Christ is your Healer. It's you, the Bible, Jesus, and the Holy Ghost.

Make up your mind right now that Jesus is your personal Healer. You were born into the family of God when you accepted Jesus as your personal Savior. He has been the Savior of the world for 2,000 years, but it did not benefit you until you made Him your personal Savior. Jesus is the Healer. But knowing that will not help you until you accept Him as your personal Healer.

You receive Jesus as your Healer by faith. You do it the same way you received forgiveness from your sins when you first trusted Jesus. How did you know you were forgiven? Did the guilt leave? Did you have a deep sense of peace? Did the guilt try to return? It often does. Did you claim 1 John 1:9? It says, "If we confess our sins, he is faithful and just to forgive us our sins, and to cleanse us from all unrighteousness." If you claimed that—and continued to claim that—you were eventually established in the truth of your salvation. At that point, no demon from hell could talk you out of your faith in Jesus as your Savior.

The same process applies to developing your faith in Jesus as your personal Healer. When doubts come, claim 1 Peter 2:24 that says, "Who his own self bare our sins in his own body on the tree, that we, being dead to sins, should live unto righteousness: by whose stripes ye were healed."

Put Jesus in the *now* in your life. Talk like He's healing you *right now*. Talk that way all the time, for the rest of your life. You can live without sickness and disease. God doesn't want you to be sick. The healing power of the Lord Jesus Christ is a gift of the Church. It is a free gift to the Church. It is a gift that is given to *you* to take care of any kind of affliction or infirmity you have.

Now pay close attention. Unless you believe, recognize, and are willing to confess that Jesus is your Healer, you'll never be healed. You may get a touch of God's healing power through somebody else, but it won't last. Unless you're a person who will tell people that Jesus is your Healer, and not be ashamed of it, that same affliction will come back on you. Lazy people never stay healed—never.

You overcome by the blood of the Lamb and by the word of your testimony. You don't overcome by the word of somebody else's testimony!

If the Lord Jesus Christ heals you only one time by His mighty power, He expects you to tell people about that healing for the rest of your life. You may tell it so many times that you get sick and tired of telling it. The members of your church might get tired of hearing it all the time, too. Do you remember somebody at your church who tells the same thing over and over again? When someone testifies the tenth time you kind of nonchalantly go, "I've heard that same story over and over again for ten years." Change your attitude! The first time you heard it you probably liked it. By the tenth time you ought to be shouting and rejoicing, not making fun of what God has done!

⏻ Prayer

Right now, I receive God's healing power to do His work in me in Jesus' name. I receive God's love in me to do His work for me that I need right now. I command my mind not to be confused. I claim the peace of God.

I say my body is strong and not weak. I say my spirit is receptive to God's Word and God's power. I'm God's child. I claim God's best through the power of the ministry gifts of the Holy Spirit.

Thank You, Jesus, for 1 Corinthians 12. Thank You, Jesus, for the gifts of healings. They are a gift to the Church.

---- **Chapter 11** ----

Working of Miracles

God has a gift that is given to the Church called the working of miracles. Yet, I've visited all kinds of churches across the country, and, as a whole, the Church knows less about the gift of the working of miracles than any other gift of the Holy Spirit.

What is the working of miracles? It's a power gift! Power from God is sent from heaven to earth to do something that's beyond the natural thinking of man. When God performs a miracle—a supernatural miracle—it's so hard for a human being to believe it. But I've got news for you, my brothers and sisters. When God says He has a gift for the Church called the working of miracles, He means working of *miracles*.

He'll work a miracle for you any way you need it, not just in the healing line. He'll work a miracle for you on Tuesday afternoon while you're downtown at work, in the grocery store, or sitting at home. God's power will perform a miracle when it's impossible to do it. That kind of power is available for the believer, but you have to believe it.

Getting God's Power to Work for You

How can you get it to work for you? First you must believe that Jesus is a miracle worker, and you must believe He is a miracle worker for you. If you don't believe that, it won't work for you.

The working of a miracle by God's power is an explosion of power from heaven to perform a miracle from God that's impossible for man to do. If you want to know the truth, it's impossible for the mind to understand a miracle. The only reason a person ever gets confused where God is concerned is that he's trying to figure everything out. I've got news for you. You can't figure everything out!

Can you go out into your yard where the flowers are blooming and figure out how that flower blooms? No, you can't. In fact, you can't figure out very much about God at all. Just believe it, that's all. I mean believe it!

Believe in Miracles and Enjoy the Results

Years ago I got a letter from a psychiatrist I had ministered to at a university campus meeting. He said, "If you hear of anybody who wants a Christian, Spirit-filled, praying-for-the-sick, casting-out-devils psychiatrist, let me know. My daughter gave her life to Jesus, and she's worse than I am. She just believes God for everything."

He said that she and her husband were out in a field and her child fell into a well. It was built up high, and there wasn't any way they could reach over and grab the child's hand. They were desperate. They looked for something to stand on, but there wasn't anything. So they just said, "God loves us, and God is our helper. We look to God. Thank You, Lord."

They looked around again, and all the sudden, there was a big rock, just high enough to stand on and reach down and get the child's hand and pull him out. The rock wasn't there before.

Do you believe Jesus is the Son of God? Then you're special to God. You're a member of His Church. You have a right to anything that's in the Bible, and the gift of working of miracles is in the Bible! Do you want Jesus to perform a miracle for you? Just say, "Jesus, I believe You're a miracle worker. I believe God's power is available to perform a miracle for me."

God doesn't work on maybes. God works for believers. At a time when things get desperate, you can't get shook up. You've got to stand with patience and steadfastness and say, "God is a miracle worker for me. If I need something, He'll give it to me." You have to say that. You have to believe that. If you don't, you'll never see a miracle.

Now concerning spiritual gifts brethren, I would not have you ignorant.

1 Corinthians 12:1

Look at that, Church! God doesn't bless ignorance! As long as you remain ignorant of the gift of working of miracles, you'll never have one. Get it out of your mind that God won't perform a miracle for you because He will. In fact, before you die, you will need God to perform some miracles for you. But just because you need it doesn't mean you'll ever get it. Most Christians don't, you know. But if you believe it, God will perform it for you.

I was teaching one night at a church in Baton Rouge, Louisiana. It was a missionary church with a couple of thousand people there. I was teaching, when all of a sudden, about 15 rows back, five or six people stood and began to talk excitedly.

"What's happened back there? What's wrong?" I asked.

"A crippled girl just got healed!" they said.

I saw a little girl standing up. The Spirit of God was all over her. I said, "Come down here!"

When I said that, she just walked out and walked down there. I had no idea that she had come on crutches. I didn't know her high school brother helped her get in there. I didn't know anything about it at all. Nobody had prayed for her. She came walking down the aisle crying and trembling and looked perfectly normal to me.

Right beside her was a boy who looked to be 16 or 17 years of age walking beside her looking at her legs. He was yelling, "This is my crippled sister. I helped her get here. I helped her get out of the car. Folks, I'm telling you, this is my crippled sister. I helped her get in here." He was so astonished at his sister's legs being stretched out.

I said, "Come up here, honey! Just tell the congregation what Jesus did for you. What happened to you?"

"I don't know," she said. "I was crippled when I came here. This is my brother, and he helps me get out of the car and in places. I was just sitting there, and all the sudden my legs began to turn warm. Then, it wasn't very long until they began to turn hot. When that happened, I felt strength come into my legs. I reached down and pushed myself up. When I did, both legs went completely normal. They straightened out totally! Then, I just stood up!"

Everybody around the church knew that girl was crippled. They'd known her for a long time. All the sudden, she was standing there, tears flowing out of her eyes. It kind of shakes people up. She was walking just as normally as anybody else. God made both legs completely normal. That's a miracle!

Elisha's Faith

In the Old Testament, Elisha believed God would perform a miracle for him, and God did.

And the sons of the prophets said unto Elisha, Behold now, the place where we dwell with thee is too strait for us.

Let us go, we pray thee, unto Jordan, and take thence every man a beam, and let us make a place there, where we may dwell. And he answered, Go ye.

And one said, Be content, I pray thee, and go with thy servants. And he answered, I will go.

So he went with them. And when they came to Jordan, they cut down wood.

But as one was felling a beam, the ax head fell into the water: and he cried, and said, Alas, master! for it was borrowed.

And the man of God said, Where fell it? And he shewed him the place. And he cut down a stick, and cast it in thither, and the iron did swim.

2 Kings 6:1–6

Look what the man of God did. If you're a born-again man or woman of God, you have the same rights. God put things in the Bible for you to believe for yourself. The Bible works for *you*.

And the man of God said, Where fell it? And he shewed him the place.

2 Kings 6:6

Now by the mind of the Holy Spirit, Elisha cut a stick, threw it into the water, and the ax head floated to the top. Some people know God's power can reach down to the bottom of the Jordan River and make an ax head come to the top of the water floating. But if you're like most people, your mind is telling you right now, *I can't believe that.* Of course, your mind can't believe that, but you don't believe the Bible with your mind.

The Bible says:

But the natural man receiveth not the things of the Spirit of God: for they are foolishness unto him: neither can he know them . . . .

Corinthians 2:14

Let me add something to that. Neither can he enjoy them.

And the iron did swim. Therefore, said he, Take it up to thee. And he put out his hand, and took it.

Kings 6:6–7

"Do you mean God just raised it up off the bottom and let it float where they could just reach out and get it?" That's right! Why? They were building a house and only had one ax. It fell in the water, and they were desperate.

I want you to see that Elisha didn't get shook up. He had faith in the miracle-working power of God. He just cut a stick, threw it there in the water, and the ax head started swimming.

Your mind is asking, *Why did he cut a stick?* I don't know. Why did Jesus put the mud on the blind man's eyes and tell him to go wash it off? I don't know. There's no use trying to figure it out! You can't understand why God does things. He just does them.

God has His own ways of doing things. He takes believers step by step. If you aren't willing to take the first step and do what He tells you, then you'll never enjoy the big things of God. You will never enjoy the victory, and you won't see many victories either, because you're trying to figure God out in your mind. The natural man doesn't understand the things of God. When you're dealing with God, you're dealing with supernatural power. You're not dealing with the natural. You're dealing with God Almighty Himself.

Balaam's Figuring

Now let's look at a Bible example of a man who tried to figure things out for himself.

God came and tried to get Balaam to go with certain people. He didn't want to do it. Instead, he got up the next day, hopped on his donkey, and started down the road. God told him what to do, but he decided to do his own thing.

God sent an angel with a sword, and the angel stood in the middle of the road. Well, Balaam didn't see it. He was thinking in the natural, but the donkey he was riding saw the angel. So the donkey turned off the road. A donkey's got more sense than to run into an angel with a sword. He started through a field.

Balaam started telling that dumb donkey to get back on the road, but it wouldn't do it. He started beating it. Three times he beat it while the angel was standing there. The donkey got three beatings because it wouldn't go against the angel of God.

In Numbers 22:28, you see the miracle God performed: "And the Lord opened the mouth of the ass, and she said unto Balaam, What have I done unto thee, that thou hast smitten me these three times?"

You might not believe that. Your mind probably wants to say, *That's pretty far out there, Norvel. I guess you want me to believe that a donkey started holding a conversation.*

That's right. When an explosion of God's power comes, God can have a donkey talk if He wants to. God doesn't have to ask you.

You say, "Well, I can't understand how a donkey could talk." You don't have to understand it. Just believe it.

Then look what happened. Balaam talks back to the donkey like it was an everyday thing. He was really mad!

And Balaam said unto the ass, Because thou hast mocked me: I would there were a sword in mine hand, for now would I kill thee.

And the ass said unto Balaam, Am I not thine ass, upon which thou hast ridden ever since I was thine unto this day? was I ever wont to do so unto thee?

Numbers 22:29-30

Balaam answered the donkey and said, "No, you've been good to me."

Then the Lord opened the eyes of Balaam, and he saw the angel of the Lord standing in the way, and his sword drawn in his hand: and he bowed down his head, and fell flat on his face. And the angel of the Lord said unto him,

Wherefore hast thou smitten thine ass these three times? behold, I went out to withstand thee, because thy way is perverse before me.

vv. 31–32

Balaam was wrong before God. When you're not led by the Spirit of God, you start going down the wrong road. When you start doing your own thing, sometimes you get so far away from God that you grieve Him because you don't believe Him.

Yet if you believe God, when you need it, a miracle is a free gift from Him. God's power is your miracle worker. It's a free gift to you, and it can even create things that you need. It can take things away and make them disappear. You can look away from something, and it's gone. Your natural mind can't understand that!

You're not supposed to try to understand with your natural mind anyway. Remember? The Bible says your natural mind can't understand the things of God.

You know, God has lots of compassion for human beings. Why? Because they're so dumb. Isn't the story of Balaam something? Balaam's donkey was more spiritual than he was.

I don't know if you know it yet or not, but where some things of God are concerned, humans are pretty ignorant about what He wants to do for you and me. All you have to do is follow His Spirit, do what He says do, and He'll perform a miracle for you.

The Orange Grove Miracle

I've got a little mission in Florida. God moved on me one morning and told me to buy a place on the side of a highway and make a mission out of it. It cost $90,000. Close to our mission, there's one subdivision called Beverly Hills, where about 7,000 retired people live.

One time when I was at the mission, God showed me an orange grove with orange trees, laid out in rows on about 25 acres. God wanted me to buy it.

A couple of years ago, a big freeze came to Florida. My orange grove was covered with snow and icicles hung from the trees. I mean limbs were hanging all the way to the ground, loaded with ripe oranges in January. My neighbor had a grove right across the street from me that was in the same condition.

If you know anything about citrus at all, you know that when that happens, you not only don't have any oranges, but you also won't have any trees. You might as well start knocking them down and planting a new grove.

In the natural, my orange grove was dead—all the trees. But I believe 1 Corinthians 12. I believe God's power will do anything for you if you can believe it. So I just pulled my car up to my orange grove and sat there in the car by myself. I was afraid to take anybody with me because I was afraid they wouldn't believe it. When you want a miracle, you've got to get all unbelief away from you. So I went out by myself.

I sat there and looked at that orange grove, icicles hanging off the branches, knowing in the natural that every tree was dead, never to bear another orange.

I said, "Lord Jesus, I obeyed You early one morning when your Spirit came upon me and told me to buy this property, start a mission, and work from door to door with these elderly people. I spent $90,000 buying this property, and I started a mission for You. And I thank You for every soul that's been saved.

"Now I believe You are a miracle worker and that Your power is available for me. I come to You, heavenly Father, in Jesus' name, and I bring this orange grove before You. I ask You to release Your miracle-working power from heaven and let it come and hover over every tree and protect it.

"I say with my mouth that my trees will live and not die because Jesus said I can have whatever I say. I believe that Your power will protect my trees. Thank You, Lord."

When I got through, I watched over the next three or four days as the sun popped out. The ice began to melt, and every orange on my trees fell off. Every leaf on my trees fell off. The same thing happened to my neighbor's trees.

I kept saying, "Thank You, Lord, for protecting my trees by Your mighty power."

About three or four weeks later it was time for the trees to start budding. Buds began to come out on all of my trees—not on one of them and not on 95 percent of them. I said buds began to come out on all of them! I sold 2,500 bushels of oranges!

My neighbor's trees had died, and every other tree around there had died—except mine! I know God loves my neighbor, but my trees lived and his died. Why? Because I believed God for a miracle.

I was in my neighbor's office one day, and he said to me, "Mr. Hayes, you know it's amazing what happened. Your trees lived and mine died. Somebody told me you went up there in the snow and prayed. Is that true?"

I said, "Oh yeah. I went up there and prayed and asked God's power to come down over my trees and perform a miracle. God's got more power than a snowstorm and the devil."

"I want to know how to do that!" he said. "Do you mind if I borrow your tapes?"

"No, go ahead. I don't mind. You just read the Bible, that's all.

You believe God is a miracle worker. It's that simple."

You see, even the orange experts can't understand what happened. But that's where God's power comes in. God releases an explosion of His power to give you a miracle if you need one and believe He's a miracle worker.

My Daughter's Hands

My daughter began to get knots all over her, especially on her hands. I couldn't do anything about it. I prayed and prayed. Then I got the surgeon to cut them off. But they came back and brought all their cousins and brothers with them. I prayed some more, and they got bigger. I prayed more, and they spread. I didn't know what to do.

But I've got news for you: Jesus knows what to do!

I was walking through my living room one night, just minding my own business, and all the sudden I went into another world. I wasn't in my living room anymore. I was in the world where God lives. He began to talk to me. He said, "How long are you going to put up with those growths on your daughter's body?"

"How long am I going to put up with them? They're not on me, Jesus."

"You're the head of this house," He said.

Some men don't realize that what happens in their house is their fault—theirs and the devil's. The Lord just plainly told me in no uncertain terms that it was my fault because my daughter had 42 knots on her body.

How could it be my fault? The devil put them there. But I had the right, the authority, the power, and Jesus' name to break his power. I had the right to throw him out and to claim a miracle from God for my daughter. The sad part of it was I hadn't done it. So as the days, weeks and months went on, her little body had become more and more covered with knots. Because of my ignorance of the gift of working of miracles and my failure to take authority over the devil in my own house, my daughter had the ugliest hands in high school.

God told me to curse those things in His name, and they would disappear. But He told me I had to believe and not doubt. The moment He said that, I began to come back into my body. Standing there in my living room, I was turning back into Norvel Hayes again. I found myself standing there weeping and shaking.

I was desperate. My daughter had been pleading with me to help her. Her hands were so ugly she was ashamed even to have a date. When I got back from talking to God, I walked in and cursed those knots in Jesus' name. I told them to die and disappear. I claimed the victory for God's power to come and give my daughter new hands, to perform a miracle for her.

You have to say what you mean. As long as you flim-flam around and shrug off your responsibility of standing boldly on God's Word, I've got news for you. You aren't going to get a thing. All you're going to do is a bunch of praying. You can be a Bible teacher, a Bible preacher, an evangelist, or anything you want, but if you don't stand on God 's Word for your own house, the devil will come in and smite your family. You have to throw the devil out. You have to get angry at the devil and claim God's power by faith.

One afternoon, I heard a noise in Zona's room, like a dresser turning over. She came running down the hallway, holding her hands in front of her, crying, "Daddy! Daddy! This scares me. This is spooky. Look at my hands. I've got new hands! I've got new hands!"

I looked, and they were the most beautiful hands I've ever seen on a 16-year-old girl. I took her little hands and held them up. They looked like they had baby skin on them, so rosy and fresh looking.

She said, "I was just standing there, Daddy, and I looked off a few seconds. When I looked back, I had new hands! I have new hands! I can understand Jesus doing something for you because you work for Him, Daddy. Do you mean to tell me Jesus loves a 16-year-old girl enough to give her new hands?"

I walked over to her and took her hands again. I said, "Yes, honey, Jesus loves 16-year-old girls enough to come to their house and give them a complete miracle of brand new hands."

I want you to know that I testify about my daughter's hands all the time. I share it whenever I get a chance. I've shared it on TV several times, and when I shared it on TV in Los Angeles, the emcee started to cry so much he just couldn't do anything. Wherever I tell it, the Spirit of God anoints and hovers over me as I tell of God's miracle for my daughter.

You see, God wants you to know and to believe He is a miracle-working God. I want you to know that you can believe the Bible for yourself. You can believe for your own miracles. When things look impossible, look to God and believe Him yourself. Just stand there because you're a child of God, saying, "I believe God!" He will release His power for you. It's an explosion of power that was great enough to cover orange trees. It's an explosion of power that can make an ax head float. It's enough power to make a donkey talk. It's enough power to create brand new hands. And it's an explosion of power that will give you whatever you need. God does it so easy.

An explosion of power came to my house to give my daughter brand new hands. Every time I share her testimony, I call her on the phone and say, "Well, honey, the Holy Ghost told me to tell them about the miracle Jesus did for your hands!"

She always asks, "Daddy, did you tell them that when Jesus gave me a miracle none of those knots ever came back?" Nothing ever came back. God is a miracle-working God.

The Working of Miracles

In one of my services in 1983, the Lord gave a little girl new feet. The doctors said she could never walk, but she walked that night!

Her parents were a Church of Christ couple who had never been to a service like that one before in their lives. They came only because somebody had nerve enough to give them a set of my tapes.

The father had said, "I believe if I could get my daughter in front of Norvel Hayes, God would heal her." He believed it before he ever came. Then he heard I was coming to the church, so he brought his daughter, and God gave her new feet. That was a miracle. The little thing just walked all around there.

Another great miracle of God happened in that same meeting. A couple in the congregation had a child who was going to have a kidney transplant the next morning. When they saw God's miracle, they said, "If God would give that little girl new feet, why does our 12-year-old son have to be cut open and have a kidney transplant? God could give him new kidneys!"

They went to the hospital, took the child, and brought him into the service down front. I walked over and laid hands on him, asking the Lord to perform a miracle for him and give him a new kidney. The couple took their son back to his hospital room.

The next morning, the doctor took another x-ray before the operation. The nurse walked into the room and asked the parents, "What's happened to this child?"

"What do you mean?" they asked.

"This child does not need an operation. He has two new kidneys!" she said.

That's the gift of the working of miracles. The Spirit confirmed the Word with signs and wonders.

Prayer

Thank You, Jesus. You are a miracle worker. The Word is true. The truth shall bring me a miracle, if I believe it. And I believe it. It's a gift, free from heaven, to the believer. It's an amount of power that explodes and comes and does the impossible.

Thank You, Jesus, for 1 Corinthians 12. I receive my miracle in Jesus' name. Thank You, Jesus, for my miracle.

Chapter 12

Prophecy

As we've seen, the nine gifts of the Spirit are recorded in the Bible by Paul through the inspiration of the Holy Ghost. God gives these gifts to the body of Christ and to individuals through the Holy Ghost living within them. God does not want you to be ignorant of these gifts.

In this chapter, we are going to take a closer look at the gift of prophecy. You may say, "I don't necessarily need prophecy." Yes, you do. The gift of prophecy will change your whole life. It's so important that you know about this gift. God had it recorded in the Bible, so you would not be ignorant of it.

Given by the Holy Ghost

You cannot prophesy just because you want to prophesy. There have been a lot of little home prayer meetings where everybody in the house prophesies. One will say something, another person will say something, and so forth. That is not the gift of prophecy. I'm not saying that the words spoken are not from God. They may come from God, but that is not the gift of prophecy in operation.

The gift of prophecy is words of English given to an individual's spirit by the Holy Ghost as the Spirit wills. These words begin to boil up out of that person's spirit supernaturally. That is when the gift of prophecy comes into operation.

The gift of prophecy edifies or builds you up in God. It builds up the Church in God. The gift of prophecy comes as the Spirit wills. If it boils up inside you and you refuse to give it out, that grieves the Lord. I have sometimes had God angry with me when I didn't want to prophesy. I have begged, "Please, God, have mercy on me." When God gives you something to prophesy He gives it to you supernaturally, and He wants His words spoken out.

The gift of prophecy brings great blessings to the whole body of Christ. You will receive profit from the manifestation of the gift of prophecy.

> **But the manifestation of the Spirit is given to every man to profit withal.**
>
> 1 Corinthians 12:7

If the gift of prophecy starts boiling up inside you in a public assembly, it's necessary you speak it out. Then again, God may never call you to prophesy in public. It can be just for your own private prayer life and used in your own family. But if the gift of prophecy operates in you, it's by the Holy Ghost who lives within you.

The Lord once told me not to prophesy in churches unless I receive the pastor's permission. I'm only telling you what He told me. But if you know it's all right for you to prophesy, then go ahead. You don't have to worry about anything when it is of God; it will work out right. The peace of God will be there, and everybody will be built up.

Be Sure It's of God

You should always be certain that the prophecy is of God because there are familiar spirits that may want you to prophesy. Familiar spirits will come and imitate prophecy. You have to watch that. If you're just thinking something in your head, don't speak it out. If it's of God, just allow it to boil up out of you. It's then that it builds up the congregation and builds you up, too.

Again, God wants the body of Christ not to be ignorant of spiritual gifts: "Now concerning spiritual gifts, brethren, I would not have you ignorant" (1 Cor. 12:1).

If God uses you in the manifestation of the gifts of healing, or the gift of faith, or some of the power gifts, you will have a good walk with God. You will become a dedicated Christian. But you will never get to the point where you don't need the gift of prophecy in your life. You should hunger after the gift of prophecy. You should never get to the point where you don't want somebody who is of God to prophesy to you. God would not have you ignorant.

What Is Prophecy?

Prophecy is when God manifests Himself supernaturally to the spirit of man. He puts words into man's spirit in a known language. Prophecy is used by God to bring a great message.

Prophecy is not manifested in the same way as the gift of tongues and interpretation. If you are to prophesy, God gives words to you in a known language. It comes out of your spirit supernaturally as it is given to you by the Spirit of God. When God chooses to use an individual, He releases His power into that person's spirit. He creates words in a known language.

Notice another difference. There is the ministry office of a prophet, and there are those God chooses to have prophesy at times. Brother Hagin was a true prophet of God, divinely called of God to prophesy to the body of Christ. If he didn't prophesy, he was in trouble with God. He got into trouble with God once because he refused to prophesy so much. Sometimes God put several words in Brother Hagin's spirit. At other times, He only gave him two or three words, and he had to step out in faith to receive the rest of the prophecy.

I'm not called to prophesy like Brother Hagin. I'm called to be a Bible teacher. Even though the gift of prophecy operates through me at times, I may go for a month and never prophesy. At other times, the gift of prophecy will come upon me, and I will prophesy several times in one week. Again, it's all as the Spirit wills.

The gift of prophecy comes to me in three ways.

1. God Himself will put words in my spirit supernaturally, and it will come out of my spirit like an explosion, full of power.

2. Other times, liked it happened to Brother Hagin, I will only receive two or three words, and I have to step out in faith.

3. Sometimes the Holy Ghost will use anointed songs or preaching of the gospel to give me a prophecy. I will be sitting there listening, then all of a sudden God will give me the whole prophecy, from beginning to end, supernaturally.

I have learned that when God does that it is always to build up the congregation. It is always given to complement the message. Usually the prophecy will contain the scriptures the person is speaking or will complement them.

Sometimes I will begin to see a picture, like a mini-vision. The prophecy will begin to boil up out of my spirit, and I will speak out what I see in the picture. Nobody knows that I have seen anything except me.

Prophecy and Visions

A vision is a scene or picture God shows an individual by His Spirit that the individual has never seen before. The scenes are given to the individual supernaturally by the Spirit of God. When this happens to me, two gifts of the Spirit are involved through the vision—the word of knowledge and the gift of prophecy.

On that day when God sent me to Howard University that I described in chapter 1—the day I had the vision of revival—the Spirit of prophecy came upon me in the form of a vision. As I sat there on the stage, I got a message down in my belly or my spirit. The Holy Ghost can give you a message in your spirit when it is prophecy in known words. Prophecy is words in a known language that you understand, flowing out of your innermost being and building the congregation up. I began to get a prophecy for that particular congregation.

Remember, if the Spirit of God comes on you to do something in a public service, you can hold it. If it is not the Lord, you can't hold it. I have sat on platforms for more than an hour with the Spirit of prophecy rolling on the inside of me, waiting for the first opening to come so I could give it out. If it's from God, you will sit still and wait. It won't leave. You must wait upon the Lord and wait for the right time.

The Gift of Prophecy in Operation

Several years ago, I was sitting on the platform at a meeting in Indiana. I was getting ready to teach the Bible when I looked up and saw Brother Hagin and his wife walk in. We went to the parsonage after the service. Brother Hagin was talking to the pastor while I was talking to his wife, Oretha. I had no idea that anything was going to happen.

Oretha said, "You know, the Lord wants to use us, Brother Norvel, to bless a few young fellows and young women who have been called into the ministry. We feel like the Lord is going to give us a room that will hold 20 or 30—never more than 40 or 50—chosen vessels God has anointed to preach the gospel. God wants us to share our knowledge of Him and what we've learned over the years."

Suddenly, as Mrs. Hagin was talking to me, I began to see something in my spirit. I saw a campus—not just two or three buildings, but many buildings, acres and acres of ground. The vision of that campus started boiling up out of me, and I just spoke it out right there.

That got Sister Hagin's attention! In fact, it so shocked her that when I finished she shook her head. She believed it, but she started to rebel against it. She said, "Oh no! Oh no, Norvel! We don't want anything like that! We just want one little room somewhere!"

I said, "Oretha, it doesn't make any difference what you want. That's what you're going to get, anyway."

She said, "Oh no!"

I said, "Look for a campus. It's coming."

Of course, Brother Hagin had not even dreamed about RHEMA Bible Training Center, much less believed he would be in charge of the campus. He thought he would get a little room and train a few people who were anointed of God. But I saw RHEMA Bible Training Center on the inside of me.

A few years later I was walking across the campus with Brother Hagin and he said, "Well, Brother Norvel, see all this going up here. This is what you saw."

I said, "Not all of it, Brother Hagin, you're just getting started real good." I saw it all before it ever happened—through the gift of prophecy. Now that prophecy is a reality.

The Importance of the Gift of Prophecy

In Old Testament times most prophecy was foretelling, but in New Testament times God not only uses prophecy to foretell but also to build up the Church. The body of Christ longs to hear from God, and the gift of prophecy is an important way God talks to His Spirit-filled children. The gift of prophecy is given to build up or edify the Church, and the New Testament church needs to be built up. That's why you need to go to church every time the doors are open.

How does the gift of prophecy work, and what is the importance of it? I will give you a personal example.

Several years ago, I set up a meeting for Brother Hagin in Cleveland, Tennessee. At that time I owned six different restaurant businesses. Everything was going fine, and I was having no financial problems.

Brother Hagin was speaking one night, and I sat in the congregation because I liked to be fed when people like Brother Hagin came around. As he was speaking, he suddenly stopped teaching and began to prophesy. I don't remember everything he said, but it all came to pass long ago.

In the middle of the prophecy, Brother Hagin called my name. The moment he called my name, the Spirit of God came on me. It was like somebody just knocked me out of the world I was living in. I began to weep and weep and weep.

God said to me through Brother Hagin, "The enemy is going to attack your finances, and a dark cloud will come upon your finances. But if you will keep working for Me and be faithful and pray and pray and pray and pray, you will come out of the attack. I will bring you out of the attack of the enemy, and you will be more financially successful than you have ever been."

I said, "Attack my finances? I don't have any financial problems." Along with the six restaurants, I owned a manufacturing company and a sales distributing company. I was making several thousand dollars a week, mostly from the distributing business.

Yet, about six months later it was as if the sky fell on me. All of the sudden, three of my restaurants weren't making any money at all. Then the Holy Ghost told me to check the books of my manufacturing company. I discovered hundreds of orders were just sitting there unfilled. They were supposed to have been shipped out a month before. When I checked on the bank deposits, I learned my secretary had stolen thousands of dollars. I could see I needed money even to get the orders out that were laying there.

Then I remembered what Brother Hagin had prophesied that the devil would attack my finances and a dark cloud would come upon me. The Lord had said, "If you will pray and pray and pray, you will come through it. And I will make you more financially successful than you have ever been."

My lawyer suggested that I sell the corporation, so I sold the manufacturing company and got another factory in Memphis, Tennessee, to produce all of my business. I still owned my distributing company, and because I produced so much income through it, I couldn't give it up.

You may say, "Oh, it's a blessing to own a bunch of businesses." It's a blessing to own businesses the way mine are now, but it wasn't a blessing then. It's not a blessing if you have to get money from somewhere else to even keep them open. That is a curse. You've never had a financial curse fall on you until you work all month and then have to borrow money to keep the business going.

This went on for about three years. I kept on praying and praying and praying. I kept my faith built up by praying. Finally, I asked my present secretary, "After you write your check this week, how much money do you have in the main account?" I really was ashamed to ask her.

She said, "$85." My main account should carry at least $10,000. It really should carry from $15,000 to $30,000 all the time. Only $85 was not enough to pay her next week's salary.

I said, "Mary Lou, I've got news for you! Look at that account. What does it say?"

"$85."

I said, "I see thousands and thousands of dollars. Not three or four thousand, but thousands and thousands of dollars."

I walked the floor in my office, saying, "Thank You, Jesus, for putting thousands and thousands of dollars in my account to pay all of my bills with lots of money left over to spread the gospel and buy me what I want. Glory to God! Thank You, Jesus. And, devil, I want you to know that I will keep on winning souls. I will pass out tracts on airplanes and wherever I go. Do you understand that, Satan? It makes no difference to me, I will keep going on for God. I will be keep on being faithful in Jesus' name."

I kept on speaking and giving my testimony. They would introduce me by saying, "He owns six businesses." I would think, *If you only knew! I wish I was working at Westinghouse.* However, I got up and gave my testimony and prayed for everybody. I would just walk around worshipping God, and saying, "Thank You, Lord, for sending in thousands of dollars. I speak success over all of my businesses in Jesus' name."

I Did What God Told Me to Do

After I had been confessing prosperity for about one year, I grew very strong. I said, "Listen, devil, I will keep on going for Jesus and speaking for God. I will keep doing what God wants me to do.

"Now listen to me, Satan. I will do it the rest of my life if all I ever eat are black-eyed peas and cornbread. You are a thief, and you have had it. If you think you will knock me out of the box by robbing me of a few thousand dollars, I've got news for you. I don't have dollar marks inside of me. I've got a vision of lost souls dying and going to hell, and I'm going to rescue all that I can. I will work for God if I have to preach or pass out tracts in the city dump. In fact, it makes no difference whether I speak or don't speak, Satan. I will keep on working for God."

"How did you ever get out of the situation?" you might ask. Three years later, I was holding some meetings in San Antonio. When I was getting ready to go back home, the Spirit of God suddenly fell on me. These words of prophecy began to boil up out of me: "Son, I want you to call Brother and Sister Goodwin, and call them now." The Goodwins were pastors in Pasadena, Texas, a suburb of Houston. I had not seen them for five years. In obedience to the Lord, I picked up the phone and called.

Brother Goodwin said, "Oh Brother Norvel, we haven't seen you in so long. Please don't leave until you come to see us."

While I was there, the Holy Ghost started working. Sister Goodwin spoke in tongues to me, and Brother Goodwin gave the interpretation. God said, "If you will go to Tulsa, Oklahoma, for Me, I will show you two things after you get there." At that time I only knew three people in Tulsa. One of them was Kenneth Hagin. At first I thought, *Tulsa, Oklahoma? What for?* Then I said, "All right, Lord, I'll do it."

I Passed the Test, and God Kept His Word

When God tells you something, it comes straight from heaven. It pays to listen to the Spirit of God and to obey Him. On the way to Tulsa, God moved on me and supernaturally showed me how to get my daughter saved. I put that into action when I got home.

I arrived in Tulsa and went to the Hagin's home. As we were visiting, the Lord said, "Go over and lay hands Oretha. I want to bless her." As I reached out and touched her with the end of my fingers as the Lord told me to do, Oretha fell flat onto the floor, crying and weeping. When Brother Hagin saw that, he dropped to his knees and began to pray in tongues. He did this for about an hour. After some time, the Lord told me I could go home.

Brother Hagin said, "Norvel, the Lord showed me why He sent you to Tulsa. He sent you here for two reasons. He sent you to pray for my wife and bring a blessing to her, and He told me to give you a prophecy." The same man who had prophesied to me before about a dark cloud coming upon my business was going to be used of God to prophesy to me again.

God said, "You have passed My test of faith. You have obeyed Me, son. Because you have obeyed Me, My light will shine down from heaven. It will break through all the dark clouds and shine upon you. It will shine upon your finances. And it shall come and come and come in abundance to you."

I had not seen a financial blessing in three long years. But I walked steadfastly before God. I prayed and held my faith up. I went to my office and walked back and forth across the floor saying, "Thank You, Lord, I see thousands of dollars in my bank account. Thank You, Jesus."

I owned a piece of property at that time that I had bought several years before for $13,000. About 10 days after I received that prophecy through Brother Hagin, I received a phone call from a man in Florida who wanted to buy it. I agreed to sell the property for $28,000. When I signed the papers, I had made $15,000!

Remember, I hadn't even had a $500 blessing in three years, but I had refused to waver in the midst of the storm. All of my family had left me, and I sat in my house alone for three years. But I didn't waver. Don't let anybody talk you out of going to church or getting involved with God and His gifts of the Spirit. Don't let them talk you out of casting out devils, passing out tracts, or bringing sinners to church. If you will make up your mind to work for God, you will find that He has many ways to reach you.

Together with a friend, I had bought a piece of property for $15,000. While we were in Denver, Colorado, at a Full Gospel Businessmen's Fellowship International convention, we decided to have a prayer meeting. As we were praying, my friend came over to me and said, "Norvel, the Lord wants me to give you my part of that property we own together. Fix up the papers, and I will give it to you."

After he had signed the property over to me, I received a call from a person who offered me $87,500 for it. I said, "I believe I'll take it!"

I said, "Jesus, what will I do with all this money? One day I had $85 in my bank account and now $100,000 is sitting there!"

The Lord said, "Spend it for Me, or I will take it away from you."

I said, "I will, Lord. Just show me."

He said, "I will. " He did, and I did! And the blessings began to flow.

Let me just pass this on to you. Prophecy, boiling up out of you supernaturally, will tell you where to go and what to do when you don't know where to go or what to do. I didn't know that I was supposed to call the Goodwins. How could I have known that? How was I supposed to know that God wanted me to go to Tulsa, Oklahoma, when I had my mind set on going home to Tennessee?

When prophecy comes to you from God—through someone you respect and who knows God—it can bring great blessings not only to you but to many other people.

The gift of prophecy is important. God can give you something straight from heaven. He did that for me concerning my daughter. My daughter would come home from the Playmate Club at three or four o'clock in the morning, glassy-eyed and on dope. I would say, "Zona, you came in at three o'clock in the morning. Honey, you know better than that. I didn't raise you that way, sweetheart. Don't you understand?"

God heard all that I was saying to her, and He told me that I hadn't been loving her as I was supposed to love her. He said, "I want you to tell her two things: Tell her you love her, and tell her I love her. Then I want you to shut up. When your daughter comes in, don't even ask where she has been. All that does is hurt the wound that is already there because you cannot help where she has been."

I obeyed God; I didn't even ask her where she had been. I just told her that I loved her and that God loved her. But God sent an angel into her room and brought her back to Him. I was obeying prophecy in my daughter's case.

God said, "Son, your spiritual pride is hurt. You are ashamed to have a daughter who goes to nightclubs and takes dope." This is where God really got me! He said, "I never turned against you when you were in sin. Why can't you love your own daughter while she is in darkness the way I loved you when you were in darkness? All of those sins you committed boiled up into heaven in front of Me. How do you think I felt?"

I got away from that harsh, fatherly, protective type of love and went back to the way Jesus loved me. After I had done that for six months, my daughter said, "Daddy, I am sick and tired of nightclubs. You love me so much, Daddy. I know that God is in this house. I feel protected here; I feel secure here. You didn't raise a stupid child. I know that every friend I have is a phony, and I'm just as phony as they are. But I know God. I mean I have known God. . . ."

God kept His Word concerning my daughter because I did what He told me to do. Praise the Lord!

When God Speaks, Listen

The body of Christ tends to take the gift of prophecy too lightly. When God speaks to you by His supernatural power through prophecy, you had better listen to what He is saying to you. He means what He says.

Sometimes, when the gift of prophecy boils up in you, it can be for your own benefit. However, nine times out of 10 it is to bring a word directly from God for the benefit of the entire church body. He does this to build up the Church. He never drags His children down. That's why He says in His Word, "Let the weak say, I am strong" (Joel 3:10).

First Corinthians 14 explains to the believer what God thinks about the gift of prophecy and what it does for you:

> Follow after charity, and desire spiritual gifts, but rather that
> ye may prophesy. For he that speaketh in an unknown tongue

speaketh not unto men, but unto God: for no man understandeth him; howbeit in the spirit he speaketh mysteries. But he that prophesieth speaketh unto men to edification, and exhortation, and comfort. He that speaketh in an unknown tongue edifieth himself; but he that prophesieth edifieth the church.

I would that ye all spake with tongues but rather that ye prophesied: for greater is he that prophesieth than he that speaketh with tongues, except he interpret, that the church may receive edifying.

vv. 1–5

If you study the above passage, you will know that God considers the gift of prophecy of utmost importance to His children.

The following is a prophecy the Lord gave to the people when I was ending my teaching on the gift of prophecy. It is a perfect example of how He wants to build up His people.

I will speak to you. I long to have you hear Me—to do just what I say. It will bring you blessings—blessings that I long for you to have. If only you will hearken unto My word every time I speak. I have longed for a church who would listen. I have longed just to speak to you and have you hear.

Lift up your hands, and I will enter in. Give Me all of you. Lift up your hands, and enter in to Me. Lift up your hands and touch Me. Lift up your heart. I'll meet your need. Lift up your hands, lift them up.

Oh, it is beginning. It is beginning to work. You think it is over, but it is just beginning. I desire your minds to be transformed on Me. Lift your hands, and you will see. You see, My Spirit shall not leave you. See Me in all My glory.

You will see how I love you. How I love you! How I love you. I will make you into the one I want you to be for Me. Take your rest. Take your rest in Me. Let Me do all I want to do. Learn to be just like Me.

Can't you see it is Me? Don't hold back all that needs to go. Go to My love and cling. Go to My love and cling. How can it be so good? Doesn't it feel good to be in My will?

Chapter 13

Discerning of Spirits

Some people say, "I've got the gift of discernment from the Lord," but there is no such gift in the Bible. They're really talking about the gift of discerning of spirits that we read about in 1 Corinthians 12. I'm going to teach you about this gift because God doesn't want you to be ignorant of the spirits around you, the spirits you're in business with, or the spirits you live with.

God wants you to know the spirit and the motives. The Holy Ghost will show it to you. The gift of the discerning of spirits will take you into the motives of the spirit and show you the depths of it.

Don't ever make up your mind about anything, to speak of, until you've prayed. Find out what kind of spirit you're dealing with. You can't think something is right; you must know. God will lead you. You can't just think with your head on the decisions you have to make in your life—who you will marry or go into business with or believe.

God wants you to know the spirit of those around you—people you work with, live with and deal with. God doesn't want you to be ignorant, and you don't have to be.

The gift of discerning of spirits is given to you by God "to profit withal" (1 Cor. 12:7). If you'll listen to the Holy Ghost, you'll profit, too. He'll rescue you out of many pitfalls between now and the time you go to heaven. You're just like me, my brother and sister, you're desperate for this gift. You have to have it working all the time.

Just as sure as you get to the point where you think you don't need it because you've arrived, the devil will send deceiving spirits to appear to you and manifest themselves as angels of light. They are so strong they will make you think things are just fine when they're really all wrong.

I've got news for you. I don't care how smart you are. Without the Holy Ghost, you're no match for the devil. But if you're open to the Holy Ghost, He'll give you the discerning of spirits. It will operate through you supernaturally. The Holy Ghost will speak to your spirit and let you know what kind of spirit you're dealing with. The devil doesn't put anything over on the Holy Ghost.

You don't know about a person's spirit until God shows you. You might pick up a little. But if God doesn't want you involved with someone, the Holy Ghost will come upon you and grieve your Spirit. He'll say, "No!" When the Holy Ghost says, "No!" you'd better listen.

People think that because they know God they're going to get everything, but they're not. You have to know your enemy, too. You have to know what God has given you by the Word. If you don't, the devil will wring you out like a rag.

Know the Difference Between Truth and Error

What is the purpose of discerning of spirits? The purpose of this gift is to know and discern the spirit that motivates a person, whether truth or error. God wants you to know the truth. That's the thing that sets you free from the devil's power—the truth.

The discerning of spirits will give you the truth about somebody else's spirit. Now, God doesn't show you everything about everybody's spirits. But He will show you the spirit of a person if He doesn't want you involved with that person. God wants you to know the difference between truth and error.

We are of God: he that knoweth God heareth us; he that is not of God heareth not us. Hereby know we the spirit of truth, and the spirit of error.

1 John 4:6

Because we are of God, we know the difference between the spirit of truth and the spirit of error. You better know the difference. The gift of the discerning of spirits will show you the difference. But when you start knowing the difference between truth and error, you might as well get ready for the battle.

People tell me, "I never had a battle in my life until I got baptized in the Holy Ghost. After I started praying a lot and taking authority over the devil, I began having all kinds of battles in my life."

Listen to me. You have to know God, and you have to know the devil. You have to know the plan of both and how they operate. If you start for God, get ready to fight, because the devil will try to stop you. He will do everything he can to stop you.

As long as you're not doing anything for God and you're ignorant, you're no threat to the devil. The devil won't bother you to any degree until he gets ready. He knows you're ignorant, and it doesn't make any difference anyway because you won't step out and do anything for God. He can pull all kinds of tricks on you and push you around the way he wants to. He can get you involved with all kinds of goofed-up people, and you won't know the difference. But God doesn't want you involved with goofed-up people; He only wants you to witness to them.

Paul Recognized a Deceiving Spirit

God doesn't want you to be deceived. When you listen to Him, God will take what the devil does to you, turn it around, and use it for His glory. This is exactly what happened to Paul:

> And it came to pass, as we went to prayer, a certain damsel possessed with a spirit of divination met us, which brought her masters much gain by soothsaying:
>
> The same followed Paul and us, and cried, saying, These men are the servants of the most high God, which shew unto us the way of salvation.
>
> And this did she many days. But Paul, being grieved, turned and said to the spirit, I command thee in the name of Jesus Christ to come out of her. And he came out the same hour.
>
> Acts 16:16–18

Talk about a deceiving spirit! That wouldn't be an easy spirit to spot. You would never know without the discerning of spirits. You would never know unless the Holy Ghost showed you. The devil is so deceiving. See how easy you can be deceived? She spoke the right words. But the supernatural power of God that lives in your belly can show you a spirit no matter what it says, what it does, or how it acts.

It doesn't make any difference what a human being says or does; it's no sign that a spirit of truth is involved. I know spirits that talk about Jesus all the time, saying good things. They talk about God, about salvation, about men of God, and about the things of God. They may pray for the sick, but they're as phony as a $3 bill.

Let's look at verse 16 again. This is God talking. You need to know what kind of spirit the damsel had. God explains it right here:

And it came to pass, as we went to prayer, a certain damsel possessed with a spirit of divination met us, which brought her masters much gain by soothsaying.

v. 16

She was a soothsayer. Now listen to that spirit: "The same [spirit—not a different one] followed Paul and us, and cried saying, These men are the servants of the most high God, which shew unto us the way of salvation."

Brother, you have to have the discerning of spirits to know that spirit. That's enough to deceive anybody without the Holy Ghost. But when the Holy Ghost manifests Himself, He shows you that spirit. Not only does the discerning of spirits show you the spirit, it shows you the motives of it and the condition of it—whether it is truth or error. That's how important the gift of discerning of spirits is to you.

The passage in Acts 16 says she did this for many days. "Why didn't Paul stop her?" many people ask me. Paul was close to God. He wrote about two-thirds of the New Testament, so why didn't he stop her? He didn't stop her because he couldn't stop her until the Holy Ghost showed him her spirit.

What would you do with a young lady following you around saying good things about God and you? What could Paul have done? "But he was Paul," you say. Yes, he was Paul, but he still had to have the gift of discerning of spirits in operation to discern the spirit at work. Paul couldn't make God do things. He had to wait for the Spirit of God to manifest Himself.

Now notice this: "And this did she many days. But Paul, being grieved...." In the operation of discerning of spirits, God's number one way to show you that you're dealing with a spirit of error is that your spirit will become grieved.

When He grieves your spirit, you had better do something about it or run from it. I'm warning you! When the Holy Ghost begins to grieve your spirit about somebody else's spirit, you had better witness to them. Get that spirit out of them, get them saved, and baptized in the Holy Ghost. Or you get away from them completely.

But Paul, being grieved, turned and said to the spirit, "I command thee in the name of Jesus Christ to come out of her." It came out the same hour. That happens many times. It didn't say the devil came out that minute. Sometimes when you're dealing with the devil and evil spirits, they don't come out that minute.

I'm sure Paul just turned around and said, "In the name of Jesus Christ, I command you to come out of her" and just kept on walking. I feel sure in my spirit that Paul didn't even stop and pray for her. I feel sure he just said it one time and kept on going about his business. He broke the power of that spirit. The Bible says the spirit left her in that same hour.

I have broken the power of the devil many times in people's lives and just gone about my business. I've come to somebody in the prayer line and the Lord showed me an evil spirit was bothering them. I said, "I break your power, Satan, in Jesus' name. Come out." Then I have just gone on and prayed for the other people. I've done it a lot of times. Four or five minutes later, they fall on the floor in a fit. That spirit is wrestling with them. He doesn't want to leave. I'd be down at the other end of the line praying for some other people, and the Holy Ghost would deliver them completely.

You see, I said, "In Jesus' name, you can't stay in this person. I won't let you. I'm telling you to come out." That evil spirit gets so mad because I did that. But it has to leave. Jesus will confirm the gospel with signs following.

You can't just hang around somebody who is possessed with evil spirits and demand the manifestation right at that moment. That's not the way you do it. You must have more faith than that.

In certain cases, you have to stay. I did stay for eight hours with that boy I mentioned in chapter 8, who had lost his mind and was out streaking. The reason I stayed with him eight hours and prayed was because God moved upon me supernaturally and told me to go to a shopping center in Chattanooga, Tennessee.

You have to watch that kind of thing. Maybe you don't know this, but what you do with your body affects your mind. That's why patients in the mental hospitals are all goofed up. Mental hospitals in America are full and have a waiting list. Everyone in them could be healed if somebody would recognize the evil spirit at work, and do what God says.

Now, that boy I prayed with for eight hours got delivered. After eight hours of prayer, foam began to run out of his mouth. His mind snapped back into him. He was from New Jersey, and his daddy had been driving all night to pick him up. When his daddy came in, they wanted me to talk to him.

I said, "Mister, what kind of church do you go to?"

"I go to a Bible-believing church, Mr. Hayes."

"All churches have the Bible, Mister," I said. "Do you go to a church where your pastor will invite people to come down who get confused and messed up? Does he lay his hands on them? Does he then claim the victory of God and command all foul, deceiving, confusing spirits to go in Jesus' name so that person can have victory and think straight? Does your pastor do that?"

"I don't think my pastor knows anything about that kind of stuff. I've never seen him do anything like that. What do you think I ought to do?"

"You ought to find yourself a new church and a new pastor. You might be a strong individual who could get along there with that kind of spirit. You might make it into heaven if they teach salvation. But your son doesn't have a strong spirit like yours. He has a weak spirit. He needs to be in a place where they have the ministry of the laying on of hands so God's clean holy power can go down through his mind and drive out every evil thought. Hands need to be laid on him every Sunday for the next three or four months just praying the blessings of God upon Him. Let some pastor who is filled with the Holy Ghost allow the Spirit of God to come through him and transfer into the boy."

The Spirit Will Flow

Lester Sumrall taught me about the importance of spirits flowing one to another and how certain people's spirits flowed. He didn't know he was teaching me. I didn't ask him to teach me. I got taught from him because of the condition of my own spirit.

I'd been going to his church and holding meetings for years. We even had a conference one time together. I might lay my hands on everybody during the week-long meeting.

I'd be in his office the day after the meeting was over and he'd say, "Brother Norvel, wait right here. Let me get my three sons."

He'd say to his three sons: "Get in line here, boys. I want Brother Norvel to lay his hands on you one more time before he leaves."

I'd think to myself, *I've already prayed for them and laid my hands on them two or three times since I've been here this week. I wonder why he wants me to lay hands on them again before I leave.* But I was ashamed to ask him. I didn't want to ask him.

On another trip back there he let it out. He said, "Put your hands on them, Norvel, one more time before you leave. I want the spirit you've got to go into my sons. I like the spirit you've got, Norvel. I like the spirit that God has given you. I want it to go into my sons. I want all three of my sons to have it. Lay your hands on them so that spirit will go into them. It will be transferred from you into them. Claim them for God, Norvel, when you lay hands on them. Claim them for the gospel's sake."

I would lay my hands on them and claim them for the gospel's sake. None of them ever did go out and get a job in the world. They stayed right with God all the time. They never worked one day outside of the church. They never worked one day for a salary or an hourly wage. They were trained and brought up right and have always worked in the work of the Lord, every one of them.

That's why I used to get people like Brother and Sister Hagin to come to my house and lay their hands on my daughter, Zona. I'd say to Sister Hagin, "Oretha, take Zona in your arms. Just put your arms around her."

Zona would always say, "When Sister Hagin puts her arms around me and prays for me, I feel a clean, genuine, something real going into me. I feel it flowing from her to me, when she's holding me. She's so sweet. She's real. You know, I don't trust many women, but I trust her. Sister Hagin is real, Daddy."

Brother, you know a spirit when you get around it. If it's real and straight from heaven, you know it. If you are sensitive to the Spirit and want to know the truth, God will let you know the truth. Remember what the apostle John said? We are of God (1 John 4:6). We have a right to know the difference between the spirit of truth and the spirit of error.

It Makes the Devil Mad

God will show you a spirit that is not truth. The devil doesn't want you to recognize him. It makes him mad, and he'll attack you.

That's what happened to Paul. Did he ever get into trouble when he cast the devil out of that woman? You better believe it!

And when her masters saw that the hope of their gains was gone, they caught Paul and Silas, and drew them into the marketplace unto the rulers, And brought them to the

magistrates, saying, These men, being Jews, do exceedingly trouble our city.

Acts 16:19–20

You trouble the devil, too, when you start discerning his spirits. The devil doesn't want you to recognize him. That's one reason you're desperate, sometimes, to have the gift of discerning of spirits imparted to you. One thing that the devil has in mind is for you not to recognize him. He wants to work and you not recognize him.

I'm telling you, as you start taking authority over the devil, it makes him mad. Absolutely makes him mad! Watch what happened:

And teach customs, which are not lawful for us to receive, neither to observe, being Romans. And the multitude rose up together against them: and the magistrates rent off their clothes, and commanded to beat them.

Acts 16:21–22

Because of the gift of discerning of spirits, they were in jail with stocks around them, stripes on their backs, and blood running down their backs. You might say, "I don't think I want this gift." But look at the end results when you walk with God and praise Him:

And suddenly there was a great earthquake, so that the foundations of the prison were shaken: and immediately all the doors were opened, and every one's bands were loosed.

And the keeper of the prison awaking out of his sleep, and seeing the prison doors open, he drew out his sword, and would have killed himself, supposing that the prisoners had been fled. But Paul cried with a loud voice, saying, Do thyself no harm: for we are all here.

Then he called for a light, and sprang in, and came trembling, and fell down before Paul and Silas,

And brought them out, and said, Sirs, what must I do to be saved?

And they said, Believe on the Lord Jesus Christ, and thou shalt be saved, and thy house. And they spake unto him the word of the Lord, and to all that were in his house.

And he took them the same hour of the night, and washed their stripes; and was baptized, he and all his, straightway.

And when he had brought them into his house, he set meat before them, and rejoiced, believing in God with all his house.

vv. 26–34

Reveal False Prophets

And when they had gone through the isle unto Paphos, they found a certain sorcerer, a false prophet, a Jew, whose name was Bar-jesus:

Which was with the deputy of the country, Sergius Paulus, a prudent man; who called for Barnabas and Saul, and desired to hear the word of God.

But Elymas the sorcerer (for so is his name by interpretation) withstood them, seeking to turn away the deputy from the faith.

Then Saul, (who also is called Paul,) filled with the Holy Ghost, set his eyes on him,

And said, full of all subtilty and all mischief, thou child of the devil, thou enemy of all righteousness, wilt thou not cease to pervert the right ways of the Lord?

And now, behold, the hand of the Lord is upon thee, and thou shalt be blind, not seeing the sun for a season. And immediately there fell on him a mist and a darkness; and he went about seeking some to lead him by the hand.

Then the deputy, when he saw what was done, believed, being astonished at the doctrine of the Lord.

Acts 13:6–12

Paul had the discerning of spirits manifested to him by the Holy Ghost, and he saw the man's spirit. Paul saw that he was a false prophet. That's the reason Paul talked to him like he did. When the deputy saw what was done, he believed, being astonished at the doctrine of the Lord.

Don't Be an Ignorant Child

I was sitting on the platform at a convention in Denver, Colorado, when a man was introduced. I wasn't looking at him and didn't recognize his name. I'd never heard of him in my life. He walked to the platform and started to speak. The moment I heard words coming from his mouth, the Holy Ghost jumped inside me. My spirit became grieved. The Spirit of God said to my spirit, "Phony!"

There were 50 or 60 other people sitting on the platform. Why didn't God show them? They were Spirit-filled believers who loved God. Why didn't God show the people that booked him? God won't ever give you the gift of discerning of spirits unless you're available. You have to be open to it. You have to know about 1 Corinthians 12.

Finally, the people who were booking this fellow recognized what he was. Not only did they recognize what he was, they caught him.

My brother and sister, you must have a great respect for the Holy Ghost and the gifts of the Spirit. If you don't show respect for the gift, God won't give it to you. He'll just let you glide along and live a sort of normal Christian life, just being an ignorant child of God. You see, you can be a dedicated child of God and still be ignorant. But I'm telling you, the gift of discerning of spirits is free.

The Holy Ghost who lives inside of you wants to show you the spirit of someone else when it will protect you. Don't go around suspecting everybody. Let the Holy Ghost manifest Himself.

You might ask, "How am I going to know when the Holy Ghost manifests Himself?" Your spirit will become grieved. That's God's number one way to show you somebody else's spirit. When you're around them, your spirit will become grieved. You won't feel right about the person. God doesn't want you to be tricked by any deceiving spirits.

Look at how the Holy Ghost helped Peter and John:

But there was a certain man, called Simon, which beforetime in the same city used sorcery, and bewitched the people of Samaria, giving out that himself was some great one:

To whom they all gave heed, from the least to the greatest, saying, This man is the great power of God.

Acts 8:9–10

Do you see that? "From the greatest to the least." And they believed that.

My brother and sister, make yourself available and believe 1 Corinthians 12, and that kind of junk won't be pulled on you. But if you don't believe it and don't know anything about the gift of the discerning of spirits, it can happen to you, too.

I don't want to judge people. I don't try to judge people. I don't try to judge every little move they make or every little word they say. That's not right. I'm not talking about that. That's the gift of suspicion. I'm talking about when the Holy Ghost moves inside you and gives you the gift of the discerning of spirits and shows you another person's spirit. Then, I don't care what they say, what they do, or how they act. I don't care how much they smile or how nice they are. I don't care how many times they get on the floor and pray. If their spirits are phony, they are phony.

And to him they had regard, because that of long time he had bewitched them with sorceries. But when they believed Philip preaching the things concerning the kingdom of God, and the name of Jesus Christ, they were baptized, both men and women.

Then Simon himself believed also: and when he was baptized, he continued with Philip, and wondered, beholding the miracles and signs which were done.

Now when the apostles which were at Jerusalem heard that Samaria had received the word of God, they sent unto them Peter and John: Who, when they were come down, prayed for them, that they might receive the Holy Ghost: (For as yet he was fallen upon none of them: only they were baptized in the name of the Lord Jesus.)

Then laid they their hands on them, and they received the Holy Ghost.

And when Simon saw that through laying on of the apostles' hands the Holy Ghost was given, he offered them money.

Saying, Give me also this power, that on whomsoever I lay hands, he may receive the Holy Ghost. But Peter said unto him (because the gift of discerning of spirits began operating through Peter), Thy money perish with thee, because thou hast thought that the gift of God may be purchased with money.

Thou hast neither part nor lot in this matter: for thy heart is not right in the sight of God.

Repent therefore of this thy wickedness, and pray God, if perhaps the thought of thine heart may be forgiven thee.

For I perceive that thou art in the gall of bitterness, and in the bond of iniquity.

Then answered Simon, and said, Pray ye to the Lord for me, that none of these things which ye have spoken come upon me.

Acts 8:11–24

You can't buy the Holy Ghost with money. You can't buy any part of the gospel with money. I meet preachers all over the country who say, "Norvel, I could have all kinds of money in this church. There's a man in town who has a lot of money. He wants to be one of the deacons (or assistant pastor, or song leader, or whatever). But the Holy Ghost showed me his spirit is not right, and I can't let him do it. He can come to church if he wants to, but I can't let him do it."

I'm telling you, the Lord will move upon you and give you the gift of discerning of spirits that enables you to see what others can't see. It will guard you and rescue you if you learn to make yourself available to the Holy Spirit.

Prayer

Thank You, Lord, for 1 Corinthians 12. I'm trusting the Holy Ghost to give me discerning of spirits every time the devil tries to pull a trick on me, tries to deceive me, tries to appear to me as an angel of light trying to make me think something is right that's not right.

From this day forward, the Spirit of God will rise up in me and give unto me the gift of discerning of spirits when the evil one comes and tries to rob me of the blessings, peace, contentment, and restfulness my spirit has in God. He will rescue me by the discerning of spirits from getting involved with evil and deceiving spirits. I'll keep the peace of God because the Holy Ghost will show me evil spirits as the Spirit wills.

Thank You, Jesus. I'm born again and free from the devil's power. Thank You, God, for the Holy Ghost.

Chapter 14

Gift of Tongues

Of all the gifts, the church is especially ignorant of the gift of tongues. If you do not believe in tongues, what is your excuse? You may say, "Well, I can't help it because I was born into a family that doesn't believe in tongues." I know you can't help that, but you don't have to stay like your relatives. Why would you want to stay like them? You have a chance to be like Jesus.

You have a chance to believe in and use tongues. You can open your Bible and see what the Word of God says about it. The reason you haven't believed is because you've been taught a bunch of dumb stuff instead of what the Bible says. You might say, "Well, it may not be God's will for me to speak in tongues."

Not true. The gifts of tongues is for *you*. Tongues are for every man, for "the manifestation of the Spirit is given to every man to profit withal" (1 Cor. 12:7).

If you say that you don't need the gifts of the Spirit, that is what God calls "dumb idols" coming from a dumb human. And I don't mean intellectually. You may be a professor in a university, but that is no sign that you have any sense about speaking in tongues. The gift of tongues does a whole lot of things for the body of Christ and for you personally.

Some Benefits of Tongues

There are many reasons why God included tongues in the nine gifts of the Spirit. In this chapter, we will take a closer look at some of the benefits of tongues.

The first benefit is you can worship God in the spirit. Man is a spirit and God is a Spirit. We read, "God is a Spirit: and they that worship him must worship him in spirit and in truth" (John 4:24).

A second benefit of speaking in tongues is it helps you magnify the Lord. You may ask, "What do you mean that you are supposed to magnify God in tongues? Is that scriptural?" Yes! Acts 10:46 says, "For they heard them speak with tongues, and magnify God." If you wish to magnify God, start speaking in tongues right now.

However, just worshipping and magnifying God in the spirit are not the only purposes for tongues. One of the main benefits is being able to speak directly to God through tongues or a heavenly language given to you by the Holy Spirit. The Word says, "For he that speaketh in an unknown tongue speaketh not unto men, but unto God"(1 Cor. 14:2).

What can you speak? You can speak mysteries unto God. Tongues gives you a more fluent vocabulary. In other words, you want to know what to say to God in a certain situation, but you don't have the vocabulary. As a normal human being with a natural mind, you can't think of what you want to say or how to say it. But tongues makes up for your inadequacy.

We read again, "For he that speaketh in an unknown tongue speaketh not unto men, but unto God: for no man understandeth him; howbeit in the spirit he speaketh mysteries" (1 Cor. 14:2). You don't understand the mysteries and the sounds coming out of your spirit that are put there by the Holy Ghost. Though they are mysteries to you, they are not mysteries to God. He knows exactly what you are saying.

A fifth benefit of speaking in tongues helps your infirmities. We read in Romans 8:26, "Likewise the Spirit also helpeth our infirmities: for we know not what we should pray for as we ought: but the Spirit itself maketh intercession for us with groanings which cannot be uttered."

My brother or sister, you are just like me. I don't always know what or how to pray, and neither will you. God didn't make us that smart! It says in the Word of God that the Spirit makes intercession for us because we don't know how we should pray "according to the will of God" (Rom. 8:27). What is the will of God? The Bible—God's Word.

Brother Hagin was going to hold a meeting in Cleveland, Tennessee. Two or three days before the meeting started, he came to my house to rest and have fellowship. Oretha had stayed with her mother in Texas and was planning to join us a few days later.

As Brother Hagin and I were visiting, Oretha phoned. She said, "Norvel, a pastor friend of ours here has had a severe heart attack. They say there is no hope for him. He is in the ambulance right now, and they are taking him to the hospital. Is Kenneth there?" I handed the phone to Brother Hagin, and Oretha told him what she had just told me.

That night we learned something about praying and interceding that we had not known before. We did three things and the Holy Spirit gave us a real assurance about our actions.

Number one: We both fell to the floor and broke the power of the devil over that man's body in English.

Number two: We agreed and asked the Lord to heal him in English.

Number three: We started praying in tongues. We prayed in tongues just as hard and fast as we could. After we had prayed a long, long time, the glory of the Lord came upon us.

It was then that Brother Hagin fell over on the couch and started groaning in the spirit before the Lord. Then God gave him the interpretation. Brother Hagin looked at me and said, "Brother Norvel, you know we got hold of something tonight that I never got hold of before in my life."

This comes straight from heaven, and it is scriptural. You will remember the scripture that says we have not because we ask not. It was when Brother Hagin started groaning in the Spirit before the Lord that the glory of the Lord fell upon us. He told us that we had prayed correctly and that the man would not die.

I want to know everything that I can from God. We as human beings mean well, and we love God, but sometimes we get all mixed up and do wrong things. I don't know why man wants to fight God so much. But God knows why. He said, "You know that you were Gentiles, carried away unto those dumb idols." God loves you so much that He doesn't want you having a bunch of dumb idols. He wants you to come to the place where you will just believe what His Word says.

Confess this: Jesus, I love the Bible. I am a Word person. Teach me, Lord, by Thy Word. The way you learn from God is through His Word.

The Spirit helps our infirmities. In the case of the pastor, first we broke the power of the devil over his body in English. Second, we agreed in English and asked the Lord to heal him. Third, we started praying in tongues until we felt a release in our spirits, and the Holy Spirit interceded for us with groanings that could not be uttered.

Another benefit of speaking in tongues is it brings the wonderful works of God: "Cretes and Arabians, we do hear them speak in our tongues the wonderful works of God" (Acts 2:11).

You may ask, what kind of wonderful works? All kinds of them— healings and everything. There's no telling what kind of ministry will go forth or what kind of blessings will fall on the human race in different parts of the world just by you speaking in tongues when the Holy Ghost tells you to do so.

The Wonderful Works of God

This happened to me some time ago, and it can happen to you if you're available to God. He can use you to be the one who speaks in tongues. By doing that it can bring great blessings to many people.

I was holding a meeting some years ago in Toronto, Canada. I had one of my college mission teams up there. There were seven young people in a motor home. We raised up teams in that particular church to knock on doors. Then I would take the team to do mission work in Canada. We were driving during the day and working in the churches at night.

That night at the service there were probably from 25 to 35 people. When I had finished speaking, the Spirit of God said to me, "Walk and pray in the spirit." I started walking behind the pulpit, praying in tongues. I just shut myself off from the service and continued walking and praying in tongues. After I had prayed for a long time, God's power was suddenly upon me. A woman began to weep, but I didn't know why.

The woman said, "Brother Norvel, you don't know anything about this, but my husband and I have a daughter who is in her 20s. She's a missionary overseas, working with a tribe of people. She's picked up a rare disease. We've just received word that she won't live, and we have no way to get her back home."

The lady had learned the language of the people from her daughter because the daughter had been a missionary over there for such a long time. The lady went on: "While you were speaking in tongues and walking behind the pulpit, you began to speak out the wonderful works of God and the healing power of God for my daughter in the same language of the tribe that she works with. When the note of victory came, God's healing power swept over there where she is, shot down through her body, and healed her! Glory be to God! Thank You, Jesus!"

Now, I wish to point out that I didn't know the lady's daughter, and I didn't know the language of that tribe of people. But you see, I was willing to obey God. When I began to speak out in tongues, that mother recognized the language. She knew I was speaking out the healing power of God for her daughter in that tribal language.

It is no wonder that God said speaking in tongues is a mystery. It is no wonder that Acts 2:11 said, "Cretes and Arabians, we do hear them speak in our tongues the wonderful works of God." On the day of Pentecost, the 120 were speaking in tongues. But the Arabians listened to them and said, "We hear them speaking in our language. They are Galileans, and they don't know the Arabian language. But we hear them speaking in our language the wonderful works of God."

The Holy Ghost can use you like that. If you pray in tongues, the Holy Ghost can have you speak out another language. You will not know what you're saying. But if you will obey God when He tells you to pray in tongues, you could speak out the language of a tribe of people as He starts healing the people. Amazing things can happen!

God knew that those parents were good Christian people who loved Him. He knew about their missionary daughter who had been giving her life to those people. He knew that she was dying from a rare disease, and He used me to pray in tongues for her. The Holy Ghost fell on the congregation that night, fell on me, and gave us a note of victory. Jesus healed the daughter, and she lived!

A Mighty Weapon of Intercession

Praying in tongues can also be used in a ministry of intercession for someone else. Intercession is a ministry. Let me tell you how God had me pray.

My pastor in Cleveland, Tennessee, came by my office one day. He had built several new rooms onto the church and needed some carpeting. He said, "I'm going to the rug manufacturer, and God said He wants you to go with me."

When we met with the owner of the rug company, he walked us through his plant. As they were talking together and looking at several rolls of carpeting, the word of the Lord came to me so sweetly, saying, "Walk over to the right and pray in the Spirit." So I walked over to my right and began to pray in tongues. The spirit of prayer was on me very gently. For about five minutes I walked back and forth, praying quietly in the Spirit. Then it just lifted from me.

When I walked back to where my pastor was standing, he said, "Norvel, while you were gone, this man decided to give me all of these rugs for the church. We can have it all free!" That supernatural deal came about through the prayer of intercession, praying in tongues.

If you're called to intercession, you may wake up at three 'clock some morning and begin to pray and cry and groan in the Spirit. Then all of a sudden, you may start laughing. At times you may feel pain in your body, sometimes so severe that all you can do is groan in the Spirit.

Intercession can be hard work at times. Sometimes God lets you feel the pain of another person as you are in intercession for him or her. You may have to live the life of a heart attack patient for a while. You may feel pain in your legs like a crippled man suffers. It's important you know what's taking place during those times. You must know God, know the moving of His Spirit, and realize the obligation you have to the Holy Ghost.

If God has called you to the ministry of intercession, you need to know what He wants you to do. If you're standing in intercession for someone who is suffering a heart attack, your intercession could save the person. Most of the time you won't even know who you're interceding for, but sometimes the Lord will show you who it is.

If you're called as an intercessor, sometimes you will have to pray for hours and hours and hours. Sometimes God will obligate you to pray all night long!

One day while I was in my office working, God moved on me to intercede for someone. I had to keep everybody out of my office. God showed me that I was interceding for a couple about to separate. There was conflict in their marriage, and she was about to have a baby. When intercession came upon me, I just fell over on the couch in my office and began to intercede for them.

At one point I thought I was through, so I walked out into the hall. But while I was talking to some people, it came on me again. I had to get a chair and sit down to keep from falling on the floor. Then the Holy Ghost let me know that I wasn't through interceding for them. I hadn't stayed in God's presence long enough to get the complete victory in the situation.

Getting Things Through Intercession

You can get things through intercession if God can trust you with them. Here is an example.

Lester Sumrall is one man who believes in praying more than anybody I have ever seen in my life. While I was holding a meeting in his church one time, he said, "Norvel, come with me. I want to take you for a ride."

We got into his car and drove out to a television station. Brother Sumrall said, "See that station right there? That thing shows a bunch of junk all the time, but I want that television station for God. I believe

He wants me to have it. I got you out here to pray and ask God to give it to me. You pray, and I'll agree with you."

So I started praying. I pointed at that television station and claimed it for God in Jesus' name. In two years, Brother Sumrall owned that station—debt free!

When you go to prayer like that, your inward man has to be strong enough to know what you want from God and what God wants you to have. You won't be able to do that unless you have power in the inward man.

Power to Save Lives

If I had not known about the power of the Holy Spirit for the inward man, if I had not been willing to be led by the Holy Spirit, and if I had not known the power of praying in the Spirit, there's a good chance my daughter would be dead today.

One night in my spirit, I saw my daughter Zona dead. I had no earthly idea anything was wrong with her, but in the Spirit I knew there was something very, very wrong. I went to her home, got her husband off to the side, and said, "Bob, there is something wrong with Zona, but I can't put my finger on it. Do you know of anything that's wrong with her?"

He said, "No, not for sure."

All night while I stayed in their home, I could feel in my spirit there was something seriously wrong. I said, "Zona, honey, is there something wrong? Have you got something you want to tell me?"

She said, "No." She didn't even know there was anything wrong.

The only thing I could do was pray in the Spirit. I didn't know what to pray for, but I had seen her dead. I knew I had to pray. She is the only child I have, and I didn't want her to die. I interceded for her that night.

Pleasing God

God manifested Himself through the Spirit on Zona's behalf, but you have to please God to do that. You can't please God as long as you say you don't believe in the gifts of the Spirit. If you don't put emphasis on the power of the gifts of the Spirit, the devil will blind you and run over you. You won't get the blessings of God to flow in your church or your personal life. Supernatural blessings can only flow in a place where the Word is presented and where you please God.

If you're ashamed of God's healing power, God won't heal people in your church. If you refuse to have a healing service in your church, God won't heal people there; and He won't heal your family either as long as you refuse Him and His gifts.

So many times when people die, we say, "Well, it was the Lord's will." No! No! No! It wasn't the Lord's will; the Bible is the Lord's will!

I didn't know what to pray for my daughter, but I did know God's will in the matter. I prayed in the Spirit because my inward man was strong enough to pray, and the Holy Ghost was able to work. He worked it out so that Zona could be examined by the doctor. The Holy Ghost did that—not me. The devil was planning to kill her. Had it not been for the Holy Ghost, she would have collapsed. If my spirit man had not been built up to the point that I could pray and keep her before God, she probably would have died.

The devil comes to kill people who have weak spirits. You can have a strong body, but you also need a strong spirit. If you have a weak spirit, the devil can kill you. But be encouraged! The Spirit of God is bigger and stronger than the devil! If you will obey the Spirit of the living God, He will do mighty things for you.

God doesn't answer prayers for weak people. Why? Because if they are weak, they don't believe it themselves. You have to show God what you believe, and you have to show the devil, too.

Developing Power in Your Inward Man

If you build up your inward man, you'll be able to rise up with authority, speak to the devil in Jesus' name, command him to go —and he will have to leave!

God moves by His Spirit, and He will show you many things if you will keep your spirit built up. You must have power in your inward man in order for God to work in your behalf. How do you get it? You read the Bible and feed your spirit good food every day. Then you obey the Bible; you do what God says.

With power built up in your inward man, you can come against destruction. You can make intercession in Jesus' name, and God's power will change things for you. He will change things—not part of the time but all the time!

But ye, beloved, building up yourselves on your most holy faith, praying in the Holy Ghost, Keep yourselves in the love of God, looking for the mercy of our Lord Jesus Christ unto eternal life.

Jude 20–21

When I was teaching on this subject, the following prophecy came forth through the late Rev. Buddy Harrison as he obeyed the Lord:

For it is entering into that time and place that I will show My mercy. Yes, even My grace. And you will find yourself moving forth in power. Yes, it will cause the works of God to bring forth the healing power to move into that place.

Do not hesitate; no, do not wait, or you will be too late. But enter in and say forth all that which the Spirit would bid you to say. For it will cause you to enter into a brand new day. And you will be able to walk forth in the land. And you'll be strong and cause others to stand.

So be diligent to speak the wondrous works of God. For it is speaking the Word that causes it to work. So, rejoice and know that as you speak it forth and believe it in your hearts, it shall surely come to pass.

For see, you are not aware of many times that you are standing in a place of prayer. Yes, even in the congregation, you are unaware. For your spirit does know because it is in harmony and fellowship with God. But the mind does not comprehend or enter therein.

And you will find yourself even in a place of worship in congregations throughout the land, that you will sit there, and you will be able to worship the Lord and speak in other tongues. And say, "Yes, oh, Lord, we do magnify You."

And you will find a refreshing, yes, it will be a blessing even unto you. For you will build yourself up. And you will find strength to rise within. And yes, it will cause you to be rejoicing and to be filled within.

And you will say, "Oh, bless the Lord, oh my soul, and all that is within me! It is well, for He hath accomplished all that thing, and He hath kept me from the pit of hell." And you will be able to magnify, and give thanks, glorious and well.

So that is proper. So continue on, and do that as well. But you will find yourself coming into a place in the many days ahead, and oh, don't think for a moment that it will be a thing that you will dread. But it will be a thing of the heart, where the Spirit will intercede. And, oh, that is the moment you too will meet the need.

And you will be able to enter in and say, "Oh, bless the Lord!" And the Spirit will sweep within. And you will cause your knee to bow, and there you will be able to enter therein. And you will stand in the gap. And you will take their place. And oh, it will be in that, that you will understand mercy and grace.

For you will bow down and you will declare, "Oh, my God! Oh, my soul! Oh, it doth travail. I need to be made whole." And you will see that there is in that place when you stand: fullness—fullness that should be brought to others in the land.

And oh, there will be as though you are dead in weight. And oh, it seemed that the enemy hath come, and that the Lord is too late. There will be crying, and moaning, and agony there. And you'll say, "Oh, my soul is full of despair!" And oh, it will be heavy, but as you continue on groaning there. For you see, that is where the Spirit is. He lies deep within.

And He will give forth into victory in that hour. And you'll come to that place! Oh, the victory—it shall shout in the air. And you'll catch yourself: "Ah-ha! It's done!" For that which you have spoken has been won.

You see, you declared it, because you believed it in your heart. And you said, "Oh, thanks be unto God! It is not dead. But I am alive through Jesus, my Lord! And I'm well! Oh, thanks be unto God! He hath delivered my soul from hell. Ha-ha-ha! Oh, glory to the Lamb! Oh-ho, hallelujah! I sing it in the land!"

And there will be rejoicing. Ah-ha! There's victory every-where. You see, you stood in the gap. And oh, it will not go any further than the enemy will be. You see, you have con-quered him: you are what Christ has made thee.

Do Not Neglect Praying in Tongues

We Christians should thank God for the gift of tongues and the gift of interpretation of tongues. God has given us the nine gifts of the Spirit for our benefit. We need to speak in tongues—magnifying and glorifying God Almighty and His works. In fact, we get into trouble when we forget tongues, because it leaves the gate wide open for the devil to come in.

During many meetings I've held in large churches or state conventions, the Holy Ghost has dealt with me, saying, "Son, out there in the congregation many of My children are cold and indifferent. I have saved them, and they love Me, basically. I baptized them in the Holy Ghost not 10, 15, 20, or 30 years ago. But some have not prayed in tongues for a month. Some have not prayed in tongues for six months. Some have not prayed in tongues for a year. Tongues was new and refreshing and glorious when they received it, but now it is like an everyday thing. It's like a meal to them."

Some Christians say, "Praying in tongues is like another meal to me. I eat three meals a day, and so what? Another meal. I can take a drink of water now, or I can wait an hour from now."

That is sad. God will deal with me about giving an invitation for Christians who've been baptized in the Holy Ghost but not prayed in tongues for a week, or a month, or more. It has gotten to be just an old thing to them.

Understand this! Don't ever let praying in tongues get to be an old thing to you. If you do, that's when you will fall off the cliff and wind up in a dark valley full of dry bones. Then you will wonder, *How did I end up here?* You got there because your dedication was not what it should have been. Your dedication was lacking—to God, to your prayer language, and to your prayer life.

Only people who pray get things from heaven. I love you, my brother or sister, and I'm not writing this book to play games with you. The Holy Ghost requires me to tell you the truth. If you don't pray much, you don't get very much from heaven. I can tell you that right now. If you've stopped praying in tongues, I urge you to get back into your prayer life again.

I speak in tongues probably 10 to 20 times a day. To me, praying in tongues is like breathing. It just comes naturally. I want to pray in tongues every day. I want to keep my spirit in good shape. When I open my eyes in the morning, I want to tell Jesus that I love Him. I begin to worship and praise Him right there in my bed, and I continue praying in tongues when I go through my day.

Somebody might ask, "Why do you do that?" Because the devil and his demons will try to tempt me during the day. They will try to throw problems and obstacles in my way. But praying in tongues at the start of my day makes them leave me alone.

I'm telling you—don't neglect praying in tongues. In one service I was holding, a little girl had been playing the viola. After I'd been speaking about 10 minutes, the Holy Ghost said to me, "Call that girl up here right now. Tell her that I said to play the viola, and I will heal the sick."

The girl started playing the viola, and I started speaking in tongues, just as the Lord told me to do. Sick people started coming to the front and getting healed everywhere!

"You mean by themselves?"

No! Them and God! You can't get healed without God. I'm telling you that the Lord is wonderful. He works in strange ways that the natural mind can't understand.

It's time that you start obeying the Lord and not neglect praying in tongues. Be a willing vessel. That way you will not only have victory in your own life, but God will use you. Let's obey what we've been taught now.

⏻ Prayer

Jesus, thank You for tongues and for being able to worship and magnify You and pray in the spirit. Tongues are a mystery to me, Jesus, they are not a mystery to You. You are the

Revealer and the Healer. You are the One who does the wonderful works of God by Your Spirit. Thank You, Lord.

If you have a friend or a loved one in need, call his or her name before God.

God, I bring _____ before You right now. Father, I claim Your mighty power to bring victory to my friend or loved one in Jesus' name.

Satan, take your hands off _____.

I claim victory for him or her in Jesus' name.

Now, pray in tongues for them.

If you have a personal need, say:

Heavenly Father, I come to You in Jesus' name. I claim Your power to give me complete victory. Victory is mine in Jesus' name.

Now, pray in tongues for yourself!

Glory to God! Praise God! Give Him praise and thanks!

Chapter 15

Interpretation of Tongues

The gift of the interpretation of tongues has its own unique place among the gifts of the Spirit and in the body of Christ. Nothing can take its place! Together with the gift of tongues, interpretation can be equivalent to the gift of prophecy when they are used by the Holy Ghost for the same purpose.

Although the interpretation of tongues is just as important as tongues, it doesn't do as many things. Like the gift of tongues, the interpretation of tongues is a gift of the Spirit that tells forth a message from heaven.

Someone might ask, "How does the interpretation of tongues work?" The gift of tongues and the interpretation of tongues operate supernaturally. When God has a message for the Church, He manifests Himself in a person's spirit and that person supernaturally speaks out those words in tongues. Then God gives another person English words of what was spoken in tongues—or the interpretation of it.

Both the gift of tongues and interpretation of tongues operate only as the Spirit wills. You can't make God give you a message in tongues in a public assembly. Neither can you make Him give you the interpretation of a message in tongues that has been given. It's as the Holy Spirit wills. Both the tongues and the interpretation operate by the supernatural power of God being manifested inside of you, and they have their own unique way of manifesting.

Let me say it this way. The gift of tongues is like a big brother, and the interpretation of tongues is like a little sister. A big brother can do much more than a little sister, but in God's eyes the five-year-old sister is just as important as the eighteen-year-old brother.

Interpretation of God's Will

It's important that you listen to what the Spirit of God says to you. You have to have the right message at the right time.

I was in Jackson, Mississippi, at a Full Gospel Convention as one of the speakers. Dr. Keller, who was in charge, came up to me and said, "Norvel, I don't know the reason, but the Spirit of God said to get you to speak tonight about 15 to 20 minutes before I put on the main speaker."

I got up and began to speak. I was giving a testimony about doing some street work, working with dope addicts. I was telling how I got an alcoholic saved in front of a Dairy Queen. I had been speaking about 17 minutes, when all of a sudden, tongues came forth in the congregation. It was powerful.

Kenneth Copeland, another one of the convention speakers sitting on the platform, gave the interpretation. It lasted about 22 minutes. In the interpretation Ken spoke out, he told me the reason God had found favor in me was because of my bold, uncompromising position on His Word.

God said to me through Ken, "Son, I will take you on three different manifestations. I will take you into the spirit world. I will show you and unfold to you the entire operation of the devil's kingdom and how he operates."

God did. He's taken me through the air in three different manifestations and let me float through the air. I've floated over the cities and down streets. I've floated just like a chicken hawk. He let me float through the air backward and forward—just like demons, lurking, hungry, seeking desperately, and trying to find some human being that they can live in. They're looking for a house of flesh that's made in the image of God. God showed me it was His will to teach me these things through the interpretation of a tongue.

Chapter 16

Interaction of the Gifts

Many times, you'll find that two or more gifts will work at the same time. In a split second, one, two, three, four, or five gifts could all come into operation.

For example, the word of wisdom and knowledge could operate and then God could give you the gift of faith to perform a miracle. The Holy Ghost who lives inside of you knows exactly how to do things. All nine gifts of the Spirit are free gifts to you, and if you believe in them, they will work for you.

The Gifts on Campus

Once I was asked to hold a seminar at Southern Illinois University in Carbondale, Illinois. That university with 22,000 students called me and asked if I would come and teach from the Bible twice a day. I said, "Why do you want me to come and hold a Bible seminar in a state university?"

One of the officials said, "The university is neutral. We believe in giving everybody the same chance. Our plan is to give up our class-rooms for a week to allow different people to come in and teach freely on many topics. In one room witchcraft will be taught. In another, there will be a homosexual play. One of our teachers suggested we give a classroom to Jesus. That is why we called you. We heard you were wild enough to come."

We all know I'm wild, so I went. There's no telling what I will do in a service if the Holy Ghost tells me to. I'm telling you what, I'll never forget that time in my life as long as I live. The people in Carbondale, Illinois, will never forget it either.

Some days I taught a Bible lesson, and some days I held a healing service. I'd say, "How many of you have ever seen Jesus heal someone? Well, come tomorrow night, and you'll see the Lord heal people right here." People piled in. They wanted to see that. Most of them had never seen the laying on of hands in their lives. And, of course, God healed them everywhere all over the classroom.

One day a psychiatrist at the university walked in. He is the same psychiatrist I talked about in chapter 11. He said, "My patients won't leave me alone. They said I should come over and hear you. They said, 'Doctor, we know that you're the university psychiatrist, but there's a fellow teaching in one of the classrooms who we believe knows some things that you don't know.'"

One of his patients had been really bold and told him, "I've been messed up now for about 15 years. I'm coming to you, and I'm still messed up." That shook him up.

The psychiatrist told me, "Mr. Hayes, I have to leave at 11:00 a.m. because I have a board meeting at the university."

I said, "Okay."

He said again, "I will stay one hour."

So at 11:00 a.m., I was teaching and nobody left. By 11:30 a.m. nobody had left. At noon nobody had left. I closed up the service a little past noon.

Afterward the psychiatrist walked up and said, "I couldn't leave. Never in my life have I heard anybody talk like you. I must say it's much more interesting than a university board meeting. Also, I must say that I have never sat two hours any place without smoking a cigarette. I must talk with you. I want an appointment with you for one hour."

"When do you want it?" I asked.

He said, "I'm the one who wants the appointment, so you name the time. I'll be there."

I told him where I was staying and said, "Meet me this afternoon at 4:00 p.m. That way after I finish talking with you, I'll have a couple of hours to pray through before I go back to the service."

"I'll be there," he said.

At 4:00 p.m., the university psychiatrist walked in and said, "I really can't believe I'm here."

"Well, you are here. I can help you if you'll let me," I said.

He stammered, "Ah, well, that's what I came for. I want you to help me."

"All right. Let me tell you, doctor, I know that you're a very intelligent man. I know you've got all those degrees. But, let me first suggest that you pull all of that intellectual knowledge out and lay it down. Just act like you don't have any sense. Act like you're a little boy wanting to learn something. I'm not sure I can answer all your questions, but I'll try. If you will, you can get delivered from yourself."

"I beg your pardon?" he said.

The next sentence rolled out of my spirit. "That way you won't have to leave your office like you've been doing for the past 20 years. You won't have to head for the country club where you sit and drink your cocktails, listen to dirty jokes, and then look at the bottom of your cocktail glass and wonder, *Is this what life is all about?*"

He gasped, "My God! I've been doing that for 20 years!"

"I know it. Sure you have. That's the reason you're messed up. That's the reason you want to ask a lot of questions."

That was the word of knowledge operating. By the Spirit, I read his life story. We spent our hour together. I ended the session with the question, "Are you coming to the service tonight?"

"Are you kidding?" he said. "I wouldn't miss it."

I spoke that night on the baptism of the Holy Spirit and healing. I gave an invitation for healing first. The psychiatrist jumped up out of his seat and ran down front. He was the first one there.

He looked at me and said, "I want to be healed."

I said, "Well, all right."

Then I gave an invitation for the baptism of the Holy Spirit. He raised his hand right in the middle of the invitation and said, "Yeah, that's me! I want that, I want more power, Mr. Hayes!"

Everybody started laughing at him. He turned around to see what they were laughing about.

I said, "Doctor, just take it easy. I guarantee as anxious as you are, you're going to get it." And he did. He got saved, healed, and baptized with the Holy Ghost all in one night because the gifts of the Holy Spirit were proclaimed.

Healing Follows All the Gifts of the Spirit

I've had God give me a word of knowledge and cause a super-natural healing. I've had God tell me to speak in tongues and cause a healing to be manifested in another country to save a person's life. God heals many people through a prophecy. The healing power of God works like a twin brother with the gift of the working of miracles. Jesus is a healing Savior and the Lord of miracles. Healing follows all the gifts of the Spirit.

God does not want you to be ignorant of any of the nine gifts of the Spirit, especially the gifts of healing. Nearly the whole world is sick, and God hates sickness. He loves people, but He hates sickness. Sickness comes from the devil. It causes you heartaches, and it costs you all of your money. Many people go broke because of diseases.

First Corinthians 12:1 says, "Now concerning spiritual gifts, brethren, I would not have you ignorant." Let me replace the words *spiritual gifts* with one of the gifts: "Now concerning *healing*, brethren, I would not have you ignorant." God does not want the Church to remain ignorant concerning healing.

Jesus is *your personal* Healer. Refuse to be ignorant. Keep your spirit and mind open to the truth. And the truth is Jesus loves you and wants to heal you. Jesus never refused to heal anybody who came to Him and asked for it. Have a hunger for healing. He will not refuse you.

Why can't people believe in healing? It's because of the way their minds and their spirits have been trained in the past. If you spent a lot of time with Jesus and watched Him, you would believe that He is your Healer. Then when you believe He's your Healer, He is. If you believe that He's your miracle worker, He is. If you believe that He will lift you out of the wheelchair, He will. He will make your crooked leg straight. Show faith. Then give action to your faith by pressing in toward Him. If you do, you will be healed.

Wonder-Working Power

I think the greatest gift of the working of miracles and the gifts of healing I've ever seen manifested happened while I was speaking in Florida. In fact, Brother Kenneth Hagin said, "Norvel, that's one of the greatest miracles I've ever seen. It's probably one of the greatest in this century." Here's the story.

In 1976, I was speaking for Ken Sumrall at the Liberty Bible College auditorium in Pensacola, Florida, one Sunday morning. There were probably about 1,000 people there. I was speaking from Matthew

16:18, "I will build my church; and the gates of hell shall not prevail against it." Then I started firing away, saying, "God has given His name, His Son's name, and His power to the Church." I kept saying over and over, "God's got power for the Church."

While I was speaking, I noticed a woman sitting at the back of the auditorium in a wheelchair. She was a scrawny, little, blind woman, all twisted up. I had never seen her before in my life, but the Lord said, "Lay your hands on her."

I asked the congregation to excuse me and headed toward the back of the church. I reached out to lay my hands on her and started to pray. The moment the ends of my fingers touched her forehead, God's power—like a whirlwind—picked her up out of the wheelchair and shot her through the air. I was standing in front of an empty wheelchair praying for it. She was gone. I was as shocked as anyone there.

By the time I turned my head to find her, she was already normal, walking, and running around. Later, she gave her testimony. She said she was a cerebral palsy case: blind, mind deranged, and pathetically crippled. Her family had placed bars around her bed. But after God touched her, her mind was sound. Every twisted, crooked limb was perfectly normal. She was running around, praising the Lord. My brother and sister, the gifts of the Spirit are for the Church.

After that miracle, the woman began holding healing meetings around the country and even sharing her testimony on TV. I'm telling you what, she got a miracle! I didn't even know God did things like that. I had never before seen God do anything like that. For years, I had watched Oral Roberts lay hands on people at his tent meetings. I knew God healed, but I had never heard of God picking up and shooting a crippled, twisted, mindless saint through the air. In an instant—a split second—He made everything about her normal.

That's what you call the gift of the working of miracles and the gifts of healing. It's a double dose. It's a gift to the Church—a gift! We would see the Holy Spirit manifest more if we would spend time in the sanctuary praying and calling Jesus a Miracle Worker and a Healer. God just loves for you to call Him a Healer. And if you will call Him a miracle worker, He will become your miracle worker. The Spirit confirms the Word.

A miracle is a gift. The gift of working of miracles is for you as the Spirit wills. But pay attention. The Holy Spirit always wills for those people who believe 1 Corinthians 12. You see, that's the beautiful part. The Spirit always wills for Bible believers! Glory be to God forever.

If you need a miracle from God and you believe that Jesus is your miracle worker, receive your miracle now! It doesn't make any difference what it is. Jesus will give you the miracle you need. It is given by the Spirit of God as the Spirit wills.

Chapter 17

The Holy Spirit Wants to Manifest Through You

People say to me sometimes, "I wish I could get myself in shape, Brother Norvel. Help me get myself in shape to receive the gifts of the Spirit to do what God wants me to do." Here's what I tell them.

You know how God got me in shape to receive the gifts of the Spirit? Fire came! The fire of God began to burn the ways of men out of me and make me a vessel His Spirit could manifest Himself through because I allowed Him to. God wants to manifest Himself through you and me more, but we have to become people who will allow Him to do it. We have to be like a piece of putty and let God mold us and do what He wants. I didn't know the fire of God could burn stuff out of me, but He sure did.

A number of years ago I was going to Augusta, Georgia. A friend of mine told me to look up some people when I got there. They were real precious people, a Church of God pastor and his wife. They insisted I stay at their house instead of checking into a motel, so I slept the night in the parsonage.

In the morning, the pastor came up to me and said, "Norvel, I've been praying, and the Lord told me that He wanted you to speak in my church on Sunday."

I said, "Pastor, I've already got my weekend planned. I'm leaving here Saturday morning and driving to the University of Georgia. I'm going to watch Tennessee beat Georgia." That was my plan because I like football. I like other sports also, but I really like college football.

"Well," he said, "I'm just telling you what the Lord told me."

"I'll come back and speak for you some other time, Pastor. I've got my weekend all planned," I said. I wanted to see Tennessee beat Georgia so bad!

He said, "Well, I'm just telling you what the Lord said."

So, I stayed another night. He came up to me on Friday night and said, "Brother Norvel, the Lord moved upon me again, and He wanted me to tell you that He wanted you to stay here at the church and speak on Sunday."

I said, "Pastor, I already told you I'll come back some other time and speak in your church. I promise."

He said, "I'm just telling you what the Lord told me."

The Lord hadn't told me not to go to the football game. But the reason God hadn't told me was because I hadn't asked Him. And I wasn't going to ask Him. I didn't have any intention of asking Him. I had already made up my mind about what I wanted to do for the weekend and here came a Full Gospel preacher trying to mess up my weekend. I thought about speaking in the pastor's church a little bit, but I wasn't sold on it. I wanted to see Tennessee beat Georgia so badly.

Saturday morning, I got up and was leaving before too long, but the pastor came up to me again. He said, "You haven't been to the church since you've been here. I want you to stop there and see our sanctuary on the way out. But you ought not to be leaving, Norvel. The Lord dealt with me again last night. He said He wants you to stay at my church and speak Sunday."

"Pastor, I've told you, I want to see Tennessee beat Georgia," I said.

"Just telling you what the Lord said," he said.

So, I opened up the trunk of my brand new wine-colored Cadillac and put my suitcase in. I went back to the bedroom to get my clothes bag and got as far as the parsonage before the pastor's wife started talking to me. I was just sitting there minding my own business when all the sudden my heart began to hurt. I started holding my chest.

"Brother Hayes, do you want us to pray for you?" she asked.

"No. . . uh. . . uh. . . everything is okay. No, that's all right," I said.

About that time, the phone rang. When she came back from answering it, she said, "Our janitor just had a heart attack down at the church—a really severe heart attack." The pastor had called and asked us to pray for him. So we did.

She hit the floor and started praying. I hit the floor by the coffee table and started praying in the living room. She was praying and praying, and I was praying and praying. While we were praying, the phone rang again.

When she got up and to answer it, all of the sudden the Holy Ghost went *bloop*, and joy began to boil out of me. I felt so good I couldn't hardly stand it. That pain I was having in my heart just left. I thought the Lord had healed him.

Then she came back in and said, "The janitor is dead." I thought, *Then what in the world was that?* (But the Lord showed me that same type of manifestation again when a girl died. He showed me that she went to heaven.)

The pastor's wife said, "He wasn't even saved, Brother Norvel. His wife is saved, but he wasn't. We never could get him saved."

The man owned the store across the street from the church. He just wanted to do the janitorial work for the church to help them, but he wasn't saved.

She asked me, "Will you go over to the store with me and tell his wife?"

"Oh, yeah, sure," I said. "When something like this happens, I don't have to leave now. Sure, I'll go with you." We got in the car and went to the store. We called the lady out from behind the counter and told her to sit down.

The pastor's wife said, "I'm going to have to tell you something. Your husband just died." The wife broke and started crying, and we started praying for her.

About the time we finished praying, the assistant pastor walked in. I was standing there talking to him when suddenly the Spirit of God came upon me and said, "Go over to the church and pray." I was standing there, just shaking in the store.

"When the pastor comes back," I said, "tell him I'll be over at the church praying. God told me to go to the church and pray."

What did God want me to go to the church and pray for? He wanted me to go to the church and pray because I didn't have much sense. God always wants you to pray, especially for yourself, when you're still goofed up.

I walked in the side door of that church. As I did, God's power moved on me. By the time I got there, He melted me to the floor. I mean, He just melted me and laid me out on the floor. I began to pray in tongues for maybe two hours about as hard and fast as I could, making intercession in tongues. Then, I got beyond tongues.

The Spirit of God began to groan through me, and the fire of God came. I could feel in my flesh, junk (including football games) being burned out of me. I felt the fire of God burning everything out of me. I laid on the floor, and the Spirit of God groaned through me for maybe two hours. After a couple more hours went by, He just stopped.

I pushed myself up to a sitting position and couldn't get up off the floor. My flesh seemed like it had things just burned out of it. I had no desire to go to a football game. It was too late anyway. Tennessee had already beaten Georgia while I was on the floor, flat on my back, groaning before God. Fire came down from the Spirit and burned football games out of me. (I think I've only been to one since then.)

Let me tell you. God can burn golf courses out of you if it keeps you away from the work of God. He can burn whatever He needs to burn out of you. Now, there's nothing wrong with playing a game of golf or other sports or other hobbies. But there is no use wasting a lot of time playing golf and going to football games if you're not going to pass out any tracts. Bottom line, God's business must come first.

If not, the fire of God can come and burn whatever out of you. Make up your mind that you'll do what God wants you to do. Say, "Jesus, help me to do what You want me to do. I love You, Jesus. I want my life to count for You. I know, Jesus, that I've only got one chance to win souls—not two. Help me to be God's man or woman—full of power, full of love, and full of holy boldness."

Brother and sister, there's nothing wrong with you today that the fire of God—the groaning of the Holy Ghost—cannot deliver you from. I don't care what it is. Groaning before God will burn the chaff out of you.

Likewise the Spirit also helpeth our infirmities: for we know not what we should pray for as we ought: but the Spirit itself maketh intercession for us with groanings which cannot be uttered. And he that searcheth the hearts knoweth what is the mind of the Spirit, because he maketh intercession for the saints according to the will of God.

Romans 8:26–27

That's what He did with tongues and groanings—made intercession for Norvel Hayes in Augusta, Georgia. For what? To get the will of God for me. What was the will of God for me? To go and see Tennessee beat Georgia in football or preach in the pastor's church on Sunday? The Holy Ghost got the will of God for me.

When I raised up and sat leaning on one arm, the pastor and the assistant pastor were sitting there. I couldn't even get up. I said, "Okay, Pastor, I'll speak in your church Sunday."

He said, "I know it."

I said, "Yeah, I guess you do."

I spoke on Sunday morning, and when I gave the invitation at about 12:30 p.m., people started running to the altar. God's Spirit started moving on the people, and they were falling on the floor under the power everywhere. Many people got blessed. As I started back to the pulpit to close the service, it was 20 minutes before 2 p.m.

A young couple who had just gotten married (about 21 years old), came down the aisle. The young man said, "We've never been in a service like this before. Mr. Hayes, we've been watching this for two hours. We know this is real. We've got sense enough to see that. My wife and me want to get saved."

Just think, if I had closed the service at 1:30, they might have gone to hell. He wasn't impressed at 1:30. He didn't get up at 1:30. He got out of his seat at 20 minutes until 2:00. The Spirit of God was trying to sell him, but he wasn't completely sold at 1:30. When a salesman comes and tries to sell you something, you're not sold until you start getting the money out of your pocket and pay him. And this man wasn't sold until 20 minutes until 2:00. Does it pay to obey the Holy Spirit?

After church, they took me out to eat with a whole bunch of people from the church. As soon as I sat down, I said, "As soon as I get through eating, I'm going to the parsonage, get my clothes, and drive back to Cleveland, Tennessee. I'm going home."

"Oh, no, you're not! I'm going to get a revival out of this," the pastor said.

"Pastor, no. No revival, Pastor," I said. "I'm not going to stay. I've got some things I have to do tomorrow morning. I'm going home."

"Oh, no, you're not," he said. "I'm going to get a revival out of this."

"I'm going home," I said.

You might ask, "What did Jesus say about it?" I don't know. I didn't ask Him. I wanted to do what I wanted to do.

Most of the time, when you come out of a service like that, you're kind of weak because you've prayed with people so long. Most of the time when you begin to eat food, you'll start gaining a little strength.

This was the only time in my life I got weaker with every bite of food I took. After I got through eating, they got me to the car. By the time they got me back to the parsonage, the pastor's wife turned the bed down. By the time they got me in bed, I was just like a rag that had been wrung out. I went off to sleep. I woke up at 5:30 p.m., and I felt like a jack rabbit.

"It's too late to go home, Brother Norvel," the pastor said. "Jesus wants you to speak tonight."

"I know it," I said. "Okay, Pastor. Okay."

The service started at 7:00 p.m. At 20 minutes until 11:00 p.m., a very well-dressed man with diamond rings on his fingers and diamond stick pins came strolling down to the altar.

He said, "This is the first time I have sat some place for four hours and didn't smoke a cigarette. I've never seen anything like this. I'd like to find God myself, but I've been married before. The wife I am living with now and I have two children. I met some Christians (I own a jewelry store over in another city), and they said if I gave my life to Jesus,

I'd have to get rid of my wife and children now. They said I'd have to go back and marry my first wife again. But I love the girl I'm married to now, and I love my little children. I don't want to give them away. That's the reason I rejected Jesus. Is that true, Mister?"

I said, "There's no use trying to unscramble an egg. Forget it. Are you willing to drop on your knees right now and ask Jesus to forgive you of all your sins and ask Him to come into your heart by faith? Are you willing to do that, Mister?"

"Yeah," he said. "I'm willing to do that."

"Show me," I said.

He looked at me, dropped on his knees, and started crying out to God for mercy and help. Right there on his knees, he gave his life to God and got saved. Just think, *What if I had closed the service at 10:30 p.m.?*

That's at least two people born again in one day. Why? Because of the fire of God—speaking in tongues, groaning before God, burning the football games out of me, and keeping me laid out on the floor. Because I didn't go to that one football game, there's a good possibility dozens—or even hundreds of people—came into the family of God.

You might say, "Well that's good, Norvel. That's good to love the Lord that much." Listen to me, brother and sister. I hate to tell you this, but I loved Jesus then, and I love Jesus now. The difference is I didn't love Jesus enough then to not go to the football game. The Holy Ghost who lives inside of me made intercession for me with groanings that cannot be uttered. He delivered me.

As a result, I have the testimony of salvation of those two young people and that man who owned the jewelry store because down from heaven come God's weapons to the Church.

I'd like to tell you there's some easy, sweet, and precious way of getting the junk out of you. But I'm sorry to tell you, brother and sister, there's not. You'll have to come the way of tongues. You'll have to come the way of groanings before God. The Holy Ghost needs to come through you and set you free. Get yourself ready to receive the gifts of the Spirit.

Pressing-In Faith

The first time I went to Jerusalem, I was to speak at a Full Gospel Business Men's convention. They put me in a suite of rooms in the Diplomat Hotel there. At 3 a.m. the first night I had ever slept in Jerusalem, God woke me. I heard His sweet, little, still voice say to me, "Get up and pray. Get up and pray."

I got out of bed and went out into the living room part of the suite. There was a little table in the room, so I knelt by it. I prayed in tongues. The Bible says to pray in the Spirit when you're not sure how to pray (Rom. 8:26). I had no earthly idea what I was to pray about. When you pray in the Spirit, you let the Spirit of God pray through you. He knows everything about everything.

After I had prayed for 30 to 45 minutes, the whole room suddenly filled with God's holy presence. It happened as quickly as you could bat your eyes. I couldn't stand it. I broke and began to weep. I wept until I was delivered from myself. What does that mean?

That means you get into God's holy presence so powerfully that your mind becomes quiet. Believe me, most humans need to quiet their minds so God can get heaven's blessing to them. It's amazing the power that's involved when you come to Him and press in.

As I lay quietly before God, the Word of the Lord came unto me. It was a gift of the Spirit called the word of knowledge. The Lord said, "Son, tomorrow when you get up to speak, I want you to tell these people, Jew and Gentile alike, that I am the living God, and there is no other. Also, son, tell them to beware of false gods."

"Okay, Lord, I will," I said.

The next day I got up and spoke. I said that Jesus is the true and living God, and there is no other. I warned all of them, Jew and Gentile alike, to beware of false gods. They listened and received from God. Then the word of the Lord came to me again, saying, "Now then, son, tomorrow I want you to teach them about faith and healing."

So the next day, I got up and taught on faith and healing. I said, "If you trust God, show Him you have faith in Him. Let your faith have action." At the end of the service, I taught on healing. I told the people, "If you believe Jesus will heal you, then show God you believe Jesus will heal you. If you want to be healed, get up out of your seat and come down in front right now. Jesus wants to heal you."

A guy lurched up out of his seat and wobbled toward the front on a twisted leg, pressing in toward the rostrum. The moment he reached the platform, he threw up his hands, let out a yell, and fell flat on the floor. I didn't know anything about him. I had never seen him before in my life. He stayed on the floor about 10 or 15 seconds. When he jumped up, he was restored. He shouted, "Jesus has healed my leg! I'm normal! I'm normal!"

Do you know why I believe Jesus did that for him? He had exactly the kind of faith the woman with the issue of blood had in Mark 5. She made up her mind that Jesus was her Healer, and she pressed through the crowd to get to Him. That's pressing-in faith—the kind that won't take "no" for an answer.

When you pray, you need to break into the presence of God with pressing-in faith. The way you do that is to worship and praise your way out of your natural state of mind until you sense His presence strongly. That way, you can hear the voice of God when it comes.

Divine Healing Power

Jesus talked to me once about His healing power and called it "divine healing power." "What does that mean?" you might ask. That means His healing power is very sacred to Him. It's a very precious thing. When it flows into you, it will drive out all diseases. It can make you totally free from disease. It can pass through you one time and straighten your crooked leg. It's amazing the amount of power that's involved.

When you come to Him and press into Him with the right kind of attitude, He releases that power. I can't make God release healing power to you. I can't make Jesus do that. But I can speak to you, teach you, get your attention, and build your faith to believe it for yourself. If I can get you to come to Jesus with sincerity, God's power will flash through you. And it's all free.

I've had the Holy Ghost weep through me because He couldn't heal someone. "What do you mean 'couldn't heal someone'?" you ask. "God can heal anyone." No, that's not true. You need a certain amount of respect for God's divine healing power. If you don't believe Jesus is your personal Healer and loves you enough to heal you and give you a miracle, you will stay in the state you are in. You will stay sick.

You need to get up every morning and scream to the heavens, "Jesus is my Healer. The healing power of God is welcome in this house. Jesus is my Healer." If you do that every day, He would heal you. He would heal anybody, but you have to do it. You can't just think about doing it and get lazy and nonchalant. It won't work. God will not accept nonchalant faith. God does not bless lazy or stingy people.

Boldly stand in front of the whole world and say, *"I believe Jesus is my Healer."* Say it again and again. God loves it. Jesus loves it. Even if you just said it because I told you to, by the time you say it about 200 times, you'll start believing it. The Holy Spirit starts rising up in you. He works with the truth. He agrees totally with Matthew, Mark, Luke, and John. If you'll think like them, the Holy Spirit will agree with you.

By His Hands

The gifts of the Spirit are the ministry of the Holy Spirit, but He uses human vessels. He used Jesus as a human vessel. Jesus was a man just like us. He was made with flesh, blood, and bones. He had to yield Himself to the Spirit of God and let the Spirit of God work through Him. It stunned and startled the people. Look at Mark 6:1-2:

> **And he went out from thence, and came into his own country; and his disciples followed him. And when the sabbath day was come, he began to teach in the synagogue: and many hearing him were astonished, saying, From whence hath this man these things? and what wisdom is this which is given unto him, that even such mighty works are wrought by his hands?**

Look closely at our text. They began to wonder, *What causes this wisdom to come to Him? What wisdom is this that such mighty works are wrought by His hands? Where does He get that kind of wisdom? We don't do such mighty works in this church. We don't do that in this synagogue.*

Where did Jesus get His wisdom? Where did the power come from? It's simple. God gave Him the wisdom and the hands to deliver the power. God chose hands to work mighty works of God so that "even such mighty works are wrought by his hands" (v. 2). God has chosen hands to be used for His mighty power to flow from one person to another person. And when God gives it to a person, it will flow from that person to you.

In the early 1970s, I was speaking to a Full Gospel Business Men's Fellowship in Pennsylvania. A man got out of his seat, walked down front, and challenged me. He was a Pentecostal leader of that city.

He said, "I didn't even know what was wrong with me until I came here. I've been deaf for over 30 years."

The word of the Lord came unto me saying, "Cast that deaf spirit out of him."

I walked over to him and said, "You foul, deaf spirit, in Jesus' name, come out of him!" The moment I said that, he fell, face first, on the floor. Hideous, goofy sounds began to come out of him. After a while, the sounds stopped, and he raised up and began to laugh. He laughed and laughed.

Finally, I said, "What are you laughing about?"

He said, "I can hear my watch tick. I've been looking at it for 30 years, but I never heard it tick before." He kept on laughing and said, "I've been looking at it for 30 years, but it sounds so funny. I didn't know it sounded like that—it sounds like it's racing."

I guess if you had never heard a watch tick and finally heard one, it would be funny to you, too. It was funny to him. He kept on laughing. I said, "Go ahead and laugh, praise God forever. Your ears are open."

Demons Like Your Flesh

The devil operates through your mind and your flesh. You can have a deaf demon in you for 30 years and still love the Lord with all your heart. The demon is not in your spirit, it's in your flesh.

Their master hates God so much. They want to get the flesh that is made in the image of God. If they go too long and can't find somebody to get into, they will live in animals for a while. But if they can, they want to get inside of a human being.

They don't get in a hurry. Demons just go backward and forward like a bunch of chicken hawks in slow motion. There are not just a few thousand of them either. There are hundreds of thousands of them in the air that don't have bodies to live in. And they want bodies to live in.

They are going to try to get your body—try, I said. They can't ever live in your body as long as you belong to God's Church and you bow down to God and worship Him. They cannot as long as you live your life for God. They cannot as long as you pray and read your Bible. Demons will never live in your body—never.

You see, demons are personalities without a body. When a particular demon gets inside of a person, that person becomes what that demon is. The longer the demon operates through that person, the stronger he gets and the more wicked the person gets.

The devil just loves to work through your flesh. He likes for you to commit adultery. He likes for you to take dope to make your flesh feel good. He likes for you to drink a bottle of Jack Daniels—a whole bottle—to make you feel good. He likes for you to eat four pieces of coconut pie and get bigger than a house. Anything the devil can do to your flesh to mess you up, that's exactly what he's going to do. And if you don't stop him from working through your flesh, then he will destroy certain parts of you.

He might pick your ears. On another person, he might pick their eyes. Or in another person he might decide to attack the liver. But I've got news for you. If you will believe that a gift of the Spirit called the gifts of healing is for you, God's mighty healing power can make one pass and heal you totally—mind, body, and spirit.

When I obeyed God in Pennsylvania that cold, winter night, that deaf demon left that precious Pentecostal. His ears popped open. When those around him saw the miracle, they jumped up out of their seats and ran down front. They reached out to me, asking me to lay my hands on them. When I reached my hands out and touched them, they fell flat on the floor.

They began to fall back into the chairs. I'd walk back through the aisles, and they'd fall between the chairs. There were more in the back who were trying to get to me. That power was on me. I walked around the room like a running machine gun and shot the whole banquet.

An old, white-headed Pentecostal missionary was there. He walked up to me and said, "Son, I haven't seen anything like this in 55 years. Back in the early days of Pentecost, I used to see the power like this. But I haven't seen anything like this in 55 years."

I could've told him I'd never seen it before in my life. But I've been seeing it ever since then. You say, "Did you pray for it, Brother Norvel?

Or did you just fellowship with the Lord?" No, it just came. I had told God I was willing to do whatever He wanted me to do.

Yield Yourselves to God

Neither yield ye your members as instruments of unrighteousness unto sin: but yield yourselves unto God, as those that are alive from the dead, and your members as instruments of righteousness unto God.

Romans 6:13

That Christmas, in a Holiday Inn ballroom in Pennsylvania, God put His healing power in my hands. It's been there ever since. I tell Him, "Lord, I'll go lay hands on anybody You tell me to. I'll buy my plane ticket and go anywhere in the world. All I want to do, Jesus, is just what You want me to do as long as You want me to do it. Then I want to come to heaven and be with You for all eternity.

"I'm not interested in doing my own thing, I just want to do what You want me to do. And I want to do it in the way that You want me to do it. I don't want to dream up a bunch of ideas and a bunch of ministries that You're not in. I'm not interested in that, God. I just want to offer myself to You. Anything I have is yours. If there's any way You want to use me, just feel free. Missions, one-on-one, TV, or anything else—it doesn't make any difference to me. Just go ahead and use me. I'm available."

Have you told God the same thing? He wants to use *you*. Look at your hands. The last eleven words Jesus spoke before He went back to heaven were, "They shall lay hands on the sick, and they shall recover" (Mark 16:18). The Spirit of God flows from one person to another person. He wants to use your hands.

Joy Inside You Means God Is Pleased

God won't shove anything down your throat. He's definitely trying to get revival to the churches, and He wants it to start and spread quickly around the world. But He wants to use you to spread it to your city.

Obedience pleases God. Sometimes the Holy Spirit blesses me with so much joy I can't even study the Bible. He bubbles up inside me with joy. Always remember that when the bubbling of joy comes from inside you, it means all of heaven is pleased. Obedience pleases God. Sometimes He demands it. At other times, He wants you to choose to be obedient because you love Him.

He wants to use you. Are you available? If you are, put out your hands to receive the healing power of God, and read the following prayer:

Heavenly Father, in Jesus' name, let Your healing power flow right now into the hands of the person reading this. I pray that it flows mightily in the name of the Lord Jesus Christ. And Lord, this person will use the wisdom of God. He or she will lay hands on sick people, and Your mighty power will heal them. In Jesus' name. Amen.

Chapter 18

The Winds of God Bring Revival

The Spirit of God ministers through His nine gifts. He melts hardened hearts and causes sinners to repent. He always knows exactly what to do to get the job done, whether He's planning a revival for one person, a whole city, or an entire nation.

Confronting Killers

I used to minister in penitentiaries a lot. At Colorado State Penitentiary, the inmates had been killing people. Several people had been killed with knives, and the officials couldn't catch the murderer. So they called me and asked if I would come and speak to these men. I agreed to come.

Before I went into the prison they took everything out of my pockets and warned me, "You may die in there. Those men have already killed several people." I said, "Well, I'm going in anyway."

The inmates began to laugh at me as soon as I walked in. I got up there and started talking about Jesus, and they just kept laughing at me. I don't mean just one or two of them. I mean they all started laughing and pointing at me. I just acted like I didn't see them. I had to shut my mind off from them, which is easier said than done. I just kept on and acted like I had a one-track mind. That lasted about 20 or 25 minutes, until God got tired of it. God gave them every chance in the world to shut up, but they didn't do it.

All the sudden, power fell on me! I'm talking about supernatural power. I wasn't a regular Bible teacher anymore, speaking with authority and teaching the Bible. Power came on me! Glory to God! He changed me into another man. I looked at them straight in the face and said, "Why are you fellows laughing at me? I'm not in prison. You're the ones who are in prison, you dummies! I came in here to give you life, so you could go to heaven and live forever. But you're sitting there laughing and making fun and heckling. God doesn't like it. God knows where you're sitting! He knows who you are! He knows exactly what happened to you! But you don't even know. You are so ignorant!"

If it had not been for the Holy Ghost, I never would have said that. But God had come on me, and I kept going: "Now, you sitting there, you're so dumb you don't even know why you raped that woman. You're 24 years old, and you raped a 60-year-old woman. You don't even know why you did that, but you got 64 years.

"You, over here, you don't even know why you robbed that bank. You're sitting here with 25 years. You're so dumb, you don't even know what made you rob the bank.

"You, why did you shoot that man? You don't even know why you shot that man! You're so ignorant, you don't even know why you're in here.

"Nearly every one of you sitting there like a little lamb is thinking, *When I get out, I'm going to be better.* No, you won't be better. You evil, hard-hearted rascal! You will be meaner! That same demon from hell that put you in here this time will put you in here again! The record says that 87 percent of you will come back again. I came to tell you how to stay out forever! Do you understand that? Now, I want you to sit there and be quiet!"

That power—the gift of faith—caused me to have supernatural faith in God and say words I wouldn't dare say without the Holy Ghost. I'm pretty bold myself, but I'm not that bold. But when the Holy Spirit comes on me, I don't see anything except victory. I forgot about some of them being killers and other types of criminals. It didn't even enter my mind. I could see nothing but victory.

There's nothing but victory in the knowledge of the Holy Ghost. He lives in you, waiting and hoping you will trust Him. If you will trust Him according to the Word, He will manifest Himself. The gift of faith gives you an abundance of power in your life to do something that God wants done. You couldn't do it before—sometimes you don't even have the knowledge of how to do it. But when God comes on you and gives you the faith, you do it.

The prison officials had already told me, "You can't give an invitation, Mr. Hayes. You can't touch anybody. And you can't call people down front."

I asked, "Well, can I say anything I want to then?" They told me that was okay. So, I had the prisoners bow their heads.

I told the whole prison, "God is looking for men with backbone. God does not want any weaklings. Any of you guys got any backbone about you? If so, bow your head and close your eyes right now." They did!

It's a good thing I had the Holy Ghost with me! I said, "Any of you who want to accept Jesus and get a brand new life, hold up your hand." As God is my witness, when I said that, one of the prisoners, a big guy who had been laughing and pointing his finger, was the first one God hit. A glory cloud came in over that prison. Those prisoners began to weep everywhere. They wept and held up their hands all over the room to get saved.

After the meeting, a prison official said, "We have a banquet set up for you. You can talk to the prisoners for one hour in another building." So, I went over there and talked to them. I was warned to meet with only two prisoners at a time because the murders had occurred when four or five people were in a group. As four of them would walk away, and one of them was left with a knife in him, lying in a pool of blood. The murderer had never been discovered.

But the whole hour I was alone with all those prisoners, they came up to me, shook hands with me, and said, "We want you to come back. You tell us the truth." "I sure appreciate those words you said." "Oh, God, what you said helped me. I could see myself."

Someone might say, "That's a pretty good prison ministry, Brother Norvel." Yes. That's the ministry of the Holy Ghost. Those men laughed at me for 20 minutes, but when the power came on me, they stopped laughing. Then they were like little lambs listening to every word. I guess they learned a little bit from me, but they learned mostly from the gifts.

You may go for months and nothing like this happens. Then, all the sudden, God can manifest the gift of faith through someone. It could cause salvation to come to one person or to thousands of people. One manifestation of the gift of faith—or any one of the gifts of the Spirit—can cause the course of one person, many people, or an entire nation to be turned. Think about this: one gift of the Spirit can change history.

Are You Available?

Are you available for the gifts of the Spirit to work through you? Would you like to have them working in your life? Are you available to stop in the middle of the sidewalk and say, "Yes, Lord!" and deliver God's message? Are you available to walk over to a woman and speak the truth to her? Are you available to deliver God's message under the gift of faith—that abundance of power that gets the job done and knocks people out of darkness by making them think straight?

If you're not available, God will never give you the gifts. You have to be available now. You have to be available to deliver God's message—what He wants done, when He wants it done, and how He wants it done. He'll try you a few times, but if you don't yield to Him and do it, He won't bother you anymore. It doesn't mean you're not a Christian, but it does mean you're just not available.

If you want God to use you, tell Him. Ask Him. If you're available for the gifts of the Spirit, God will use you to be a tremendous blessing!

⏻ Prayer

Jesus, I make myself available for the gifts. I will obey You if You want to use me like that. I will obey You in the gifts. Lord, send the power to me. Cause me to do something that's in Your will that I couldn't do before. Thank You, Lord, for the gifts of the Spirit. In Jesus's name, I receive them with thanksgiving. I accept them. And I accept being used by You as the Spirit wills, not as I will. In Jesus's name. Amen."

Is Jesus Your Savior?

The Bible says that all have sinned and come short of the glory of God (Romans 3:23). It also says that the wages of sin is death; but the gift of God is eternal life through Jesus Christ our Lord (Romans 6:23) and that Christ died for our sins (1 Corinthians 15:3).

The Bible also says, "For by grace are ye saved through faith; and that not of yourselves: it is the gift of God (Ephesians 2:8) "If thou shalt confess with thy mouth the Lord Jesus, and shalt believe in thine heart that God hath raised him from the dead, thou shalt be saved (Romans 10:9).

If you have never received Jesus as your Savior, accept Him now! Pray this pray out loud:

> **Father, I thank You that Christ died for my sins and because of that I can have eternal life with You as a free gift by believing in Him. I confess with my mouth the Lord Jesus and believe in my heart that God raised Him from the dead. I thank You, Lord, for saving me and that I will live with you for eternity! In Jesus' name, amen.**

Other Books
by Norvel Hayes

Divine Healing

Endued with Power

God's Light

How to Become a Wise Man in God's Eyes

How to Cast Out Devils

Know Your Enemy

Pleasing the Lord

Stand in the Gap for Your Children

How to Get Your Prayers Answered

What Causes Jesus to Work Miracles

Confession Brings Possession

Faith in Action

Getting to Know God

The Blessing of Obedience

Number One Way to Fight the Devil

What to Do for Healing

God's Light

Financial Dominion

God's Power through Laying on of Hands

How to Get God's Attention

How to Live and Not Die

Legacy of Faith

Putting Your Angels to Work

The Ministry for Everyone

Let Not Your Heart Be Troubled

Worship

Faith Has No Feelings

Faith to Obtain Your Inheritance

Misguided Faith

The Master Teacher

The True Riches

Why You Should Speak in Tongues

Available at www.harrisonhouse.com or any fine bookstore.

Check out
our **Harrison House**
bestsellers page at
harrisonhouse.com/bestsellers

for fresh,
faith-building messages
that will equip you
to walk in the
abundant life.

YOUR HOUSE OF

FAITH

Sign up for a **FREE** subscription to the
Harrison House digital magazine and get
excellent content delivered directly to your inbox!
harrisonhouse.com/signup

Sign up for Messages that Equip You to Walk in the Abundant Life

• Receive biblically sound and Spirit-filled encouragement to focus on and maintain your faith
• Grow in faith through biblical teachings, prayers, ar other spiritual insights
• Connect with a community of believers who share values and beliefs

Experience Fresh Teachings and Inspiration to Build Your Faith

• Deepen your understanding of God's purpose for your life
• Stay connected and inspired on your faith journey
• Learn how to grow spiritually in your walk with God

In the Right Hands, This Book Will Change Lives!

Most of the people who need this message will not be looking for this book. To change their lives, you need to **put a copy of this book in their hands.**

Our ministry is constantly seeking methods to find the people who need this anointed message to change their lives. **Will you help us reach these people?**

Extend this ministry by sowing three, five, ten, or *even more* books today and change people's lives for the better! Your generosity will be part of catalyzing the Great Awakening that many have been prophesying and praying for.

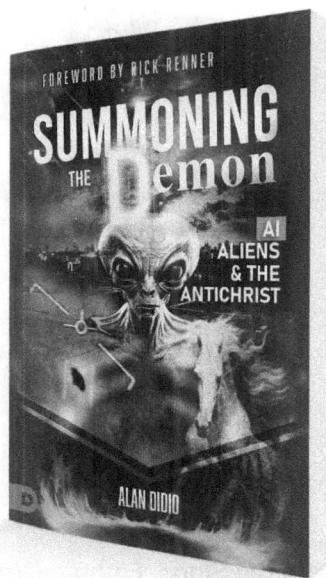

From
Alan DiDio

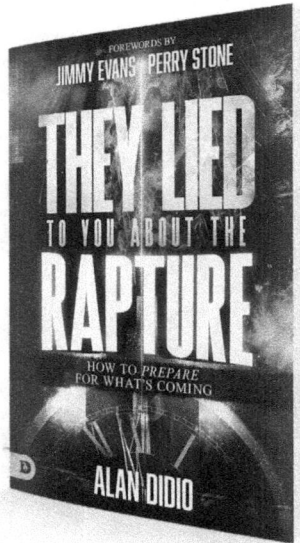

Decode the Rapture. Discern the Signs. Embrace Your End-Time Assignmen

Are you confused, frightened, or indifferent toward end times teachings about the rapture?

You're not alone.

The end-time teaching of the *rapture* has sparked controversy, misunderstandings, and debate among Christians. Some misrepresent it as an excuse to disengage from worldly affairs and await heavenly rescue. Others mock it as escapist theology, reject it outright, or live blissfully ignorant of the glory and crisis that will unfold on earth in the last days.

Alan DiDio, pastor, influential podcaster, and seasoned end times teacher, exposes false teachings and misinterpretations about the rapture, reconnecting you to a life of purpose, meaning, and Kingdom impact in these last days.

Through clear teachings and profound truths, you'll discover how to:

- **Discern prophetic signs of the times** pointing to the coming rapture.
- **Live every day** fueled by a clear sense of purpose and meaning.
- **Avoid being caught off guard** by prophecies being fulfilled around you.
- **"Occupy" your sphere of influence** by living as a representative of the Kingdom until Jesus returns.

The world may be caught off guard by the return of Jesus, but you are called to discern the tim and seasons. Open your eyes to the reality of Jesus' imminent return and live every single day filled with a sense of divine purpose and Kingdom assignment!

Purchase your copy wherever books are sold.

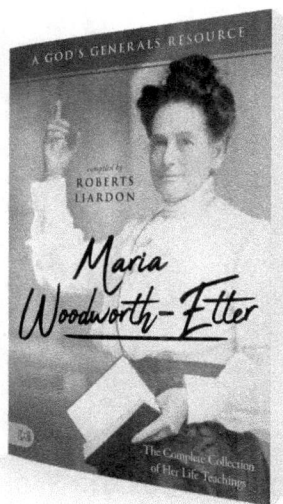

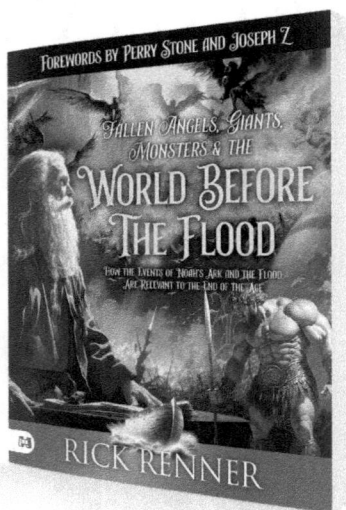

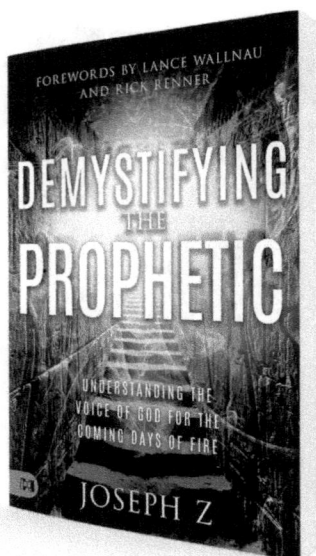

www.ingramcontent.com/pod-product-compliance
Lightning Source LLC
Chambersburg PA
CBHW070031100426
42740CB00013B/2663